Memoirs

of a

New England Village Choir.

Memoirs

of a

New England Village Choir.

with

Occasional Reflections.

by [Samuel Gilman]

New introduction by Karl Kroeger

Da Capo Press • New York • 1984

Library of Congress Cataloging in Publication Data

Gilman, Samuel, 1791-1858.
  Memoirs of a New England village choir.

  (Da Capo Press music reprint series)
  Fictionalized account of the author's
experiences while at an academy in Atkinson, N.H.,
during his youth (ca. 1805)
  Reprint. Originally published: Boston : S. G.
Goodrich, 1829.
  1. New English — History — Fiction. 2. Choirs
(Music) — New England — History — Fiction.
I. Kroeger, Karl. II. Title.
PS1744.G6M4 1984   813'.2   82-7297
ISBN 0-306-76175-0   AACR2

This Da Capo Press reprint edition of *Memoirs of a New England Choir*
is an unabridged republication of the 1829 edition published
in Boston, here supplemented with a new introduction by Karl Kroeger.

Published by Da Capo Press, Inc.
A Subsidiary of Plenum Publishing Corporation
233 Spring Street, New York, N.Y. 10013

INTRODUCTION

In many small American towns today, musical life still revolves around the church. It is the center of social and cultural activities as well as the focus of civic and religious concerns for many smaller communities. In the days before mass entertainment media and easy transportation, the village church, often separated from neighboring communities by poor roads and from major population centers by scores of miles, assumed an even more central role in the lives of the people.

During the eighteenth and early nineteenth centuries musicians in small towns were few in number and concerned, usually, with trades and commercial activities other than music. Most instrumental performers were self-taught amateurs who learned their technique from a published tutor and acquired some facility through practice in leisure hours. Singers were most often products of singing schools held now and then by itinerant singing masters who passed through the area. Musical activities in the village focused on the church, and membership in the church choir became a status symbol of considerable importance. The author, Lucy Larcom, aptly expressed this: "To stand up there and be one of the choir, seemed to me very little short of promotion to the ranks of cherubim and seraphim."[1]

[1]Lucy Larcom, *A New England Girlhood* (Boston, 1889), p. 72.

Barred from the church by the Puritan forefathers as a "popish" accretion to the Biblical Christian service of worship, the choir made a slow comeback into New England churches during the eighteenth century. The purpose of its reintroduction was a support for congregational singing, which over the preceding century had declined and evolved "into an horrid Medley of confused and disorderly Noises."[2] After a time, however, in many places the choir not only led congregational singing but undertook to perform all the music in the worship service.

Choir membership brought with it status, but to be chosen leader of the choir conferred an authority virtually unchallenged in village musical circles. It was the leader's responsibility, once the minister had selected and read a psalm or hymn, to find an appropriate tune, assign the opening pitches to the various parts, set the tempo, and by voice and gesture generally control the performance — not as a conductor but as the leading participant, such as the first violinist of a string quartet directs the ensemble with nods and gestures while playing with the group. A conscientious leader might also rehearse the choir an evening or two during the week, offering singing instruction to beginners and intermediates. So important was the leader to musical performances in small-town churches that choir members would usually not perform without him,[3] and the efforts of a substitute were often met

[2]Thomas Walter, *The Grounds and Rules of Musick Explained* (Boston, 1723), p. 2.

[3]See William Bentley, *The Diary of William Bentley, D.D.* (Gloucester, 1962), Vol. I, p. 283, entry for 7 August 1791, and Vol. III, p. 314, entry for 16 August 1807 for several instances of this in Salem, Massachusetts.

with resistance. Through the choice of music and his prestige and authority among choir members, the leader exerted an enormous influence on the musical life of the community.

During the early nineteenth century a reform movement took hold of church music in New England. Since the late 1770s American composers of psalmody had largely dominated this music. Through their activities as singing masters they had introduced into the churches music composed by themselves and their compatriots—music different in style and spirit from the psalm-tunes sung earlier in the century. Their music was more rhythmic and spirited than the staid, old psalm-tunes, and often took the form of the fuging-tune, characterized by quasi-imitative polyphony and verbal conflict between the voices.[4] In the 1790s some members of the clergy and gentlemen of refined taste began to urge the adoption of other music, claiming that the spirited fuges and fast-paced hymn-tunes, which had caught the public's fancy, were inappropriate for divine worship. Some preferred a return to the old psalm-tunes of the pre-Revolutionary War era; others opted for the mellifuous hymn-tunes currently in vogue in some English churches. Both agreed that American products were both crude in technique and inappropriate in expression and should be removed from the sanctuary. The success of their reform movement, which began slowly but gained mo-

---

[4]For a discussion of the fuging-tune, see Irving Lowens, "The Origins of the American Fuging-Tune" in his *Music and Musicians in Early America* (New York, 1964), pp. 237–248.

mentum after 1800, was such that by 1820 few tunes by American composers remained in the singing books.[5]

All of the above-mentioned activity and intercommunal relationships are presented with accuracy, sympathy, and good-natured humor in Samuel Gilman's *Memoirs of a New England Village Choir.* Although ostensibly a work of fiction, its incidents ring true and many can be supported by documentary evidence from other sources.[6] Gilman wrote about a situation he knew well through personal experience; though some details may be somewhat broadly drawn for purposes of humorous narrative, there can no doubt that the incidents did occur, if not in his pseudonymous town of Waterfield, then in other towns of that time and place.

Samuel Gilman was born in Gloucester, Massachusetts, on 16 February 1791, the son of Frederick Gilman, a prosperous merchant. In 1798 his father suffered severe business losses in the undeclared naval war with France; several of his ships were captured, and he died shortly thereafter. His widow moved to Salem, Massachusetts, but arranged for her son, Samuel, to be educated at an academy in Atkinson, New

[5]Richard Crawford discusses this reform movement in "A Hardening of the Categories" in his *American Studies and American Musicology,* I.S.A.M. Publication No. 4 (Brooklyn, 1974), pp. 16–31.

[6]For example, by numerous entries in William Bentley's diary, by N. D. Gould's *Church Music in America* (Boston, 1853), and by many lectures, sermons, and tracts published at the time.

Hampshire, taught by Rev. Stephen Peabody.[7] Gilman entered Harvard College in 1807 and graduated in 1811. After several months of work in a Boston bank, he returned to Harvard for additional training in theology. From 1812 until 1817 he taught school in Boston, and then for two years he tutored mathematics at Harvard. In December 1819 he was ordained as minister of the Second Independent Church (Unitarian) of Charleston, South Carolina. In the same month he married Caroline Howard, who later became known as an author of children's books. Samuel Gilman spent the rest of his life in Charleston, although he made frequent trips back to New England. It was during one of these trips that he died unexpectedly in Kingston, Massachusetts, on 9 February 1858.[8]

Gilman's literary activity began during his student years at Harvard and continued throughout his life. He wrote a class poem for his graduation; contributed verse, essays, and criticism to *The North American Review* while living in Boston; and in Charleston, in addition to his pastoral duties, found time to compose and publish poems, essays, sketches, and sermons written in an easy and engaging style. Although he wrote and published much, gathering what he considered to

[7]Rev. Peabody and his activities are the subject of Gilman's sketch, "Reminiscences of a New England Clergyman and his Lady," published in his *Contributions to Literature* (Boston, 1856), pp. 190–230.

[8]Biographical data was taken from *Dictionary of American Biography* (New York, 1928–36), v. 7, pp. 305–6.

be his best work into a volume entitled *Contributions to Literature* in 1856, Gilman today is remembered for only two works: the poem "Fair Harvard," written for and sung at the bicentennial celebrations of the college in 1836; and *Memoirs of a New England Village Choir,* which went through three editions[9] and was included in his *Contributions to Literature.*

Although Gilman attempted to hide locale and identities, it seems clear enough that the fictional town of Waterfield is really Atkinson, New Hampshire, and the minister, Mr. Welby, is Rev. Stephen Peabody. Other pseudonymous characters in the narrative, not so easily identified, are similarly based on real people. Gilman's descriptions are finely drawn but his satire is gentle. Characters he does not care for bear Sheridanian names such as Mr. Forehead and Mrs. Shrinknot; those he admires are called by ordinary names and treated with kindness and sympathy. The story gives many small details of musical life and interpersonal relationships within the choir. We learn, for example, that *The Village Harmony,* a popular tunebook during the first two decades of the nineteenth century, was used by the choir,[10] and we discover the names of some tunes from their repertory. We are introduced to the consequences of setting the pitch of the tune too high, or of selecting a tune in common meter for a

[9]Editions were published in 1829, 1834, and 1846.

[10]Published in Exeter, NH, *The Village Harmony* appeared in seventeen editions between 1795 and 1821. One of the most long-lived on New England tunebooks, its pages clearly reflect the progress of the reform movement in psalmody.

hymn in long meter—both surely common occurrences. We witness the petty offense taken by choir members when the minister mildly chided them, and their snobbish pride and class prejudice when one of their number dared step out of her accustomed place. But we also see their triumphs when well trained and competently led. We can only regret that the author did not make good on his promise, given in the last sentence, to write a "History of a New England Singing-School." That would have been as enlightening for that New England institution as the present volume is for the New England church choir.

— KARL KROEGER
Winston-Salem, North Carolina
September 1983

[11]English devotional verse employed three standard meters: long meter, a pattern of four lines of eight syllables each in iambic meter, common meter (8.6.8.6), and short meter (6.6.8.6). A tune designed to be sung to common-meter hymns will not contain enough music in the second and fourth phrases to fit the extra syllables in long-meter verse and problems will result.

MEMOIRS

OF A

NEW ENGLAND VILLAGE CHOIR.

WITH

OCCASIONAL REFLECTIONS.

———

BY A MEMBER.

———

What though no cherubim are here display'd,
No gilded walls, no cedar colonnade,
No crimson curtains hang around our quire,
Wrought by the ingenious artisan of Tyre;
No doors of fir on golden hinges turn;
No spicy gums in golden censers burn;
If humble love, if gratitude inspire,
One strain shall silence even the temple's quire,
And rival Michael's trump, nor yield to Gabriel's lyre.

Pierpont's Airs of Palestine.

BOSTON.—S. G. GOODRICH, AND CO.

———

1829.

MEMOIRS

OF A

NEW ENGLAND VILLAGE CHOIR.

————

PART FIRST.

THE MEETINGHOUSE.

WISHING to present a sketch of manners in New England, and of some changes that have occurred in our taste for sacred music, I have presumed to adopt for the purpose, a kind of desultory narrative.

The time when the few humble incidents occurred, which are recorded in the following pages, embraced about ten years, bordering upon the last and present centuries. The place was a village, situated not far from the river Merrimac ; and for the sake of avoiding any invidious allusions or interpretations, I shall give to the town the fictitious name of Waterfield.

1

Many years had now elapsed, since any interruption, or indeed any thing extraordinary, had happened to the music, that was barely tolerated in the meetinghouse at Waterfield. At the period when our memoirs commence, the long-established leader, Mr Pitchtone, had just removed with his family to one of the new towns in the District of Maine, and the choir, which had been for some time in a decaying state, was thus left without any head, or any hope of keeping itself together. For some Sundays after his departure, not an individual ventured to appear in the singing seats. Young Williams, the eccentric and interesting shoemaker, who was an apprentice to his father, knew perfectly well how to set the tune, but he had not as yet acquired sufficient self-confidence to pass the leading notes round to the performers of different parts, nor to encounter various other kinds of intimidating notoriety attached to the office. The female singers, besides, had been so long and so implicitly accustomed to their late leader, that nothing could have induced them to submit to the control of so young and inexperienced a guide. And as no other member of the congregation possessed sufficient skill or firmness to undertake this responsible and conspicuous task, the consequence was, that nearly all the performers, at first, absented themselves, not only from the singing gallery, but even from church. Most of them had been so long habituated to their elevated position, and their active duty in the place of worship, that they could not immediately undergo the awkwardness of sitting below among the congregation, and were not a little apprehensive of meeting the stares of mingled curiosity and reproach, which they knew would be directed towards them. In addition to these circumstances, many had not the heart to witness the embarrassment and pain which would naturally be created in the minister and his flock, by the anticipated chasm in the usual routine of worship. Two or three, however, of the more courageous in the late choir, ventured to attend church even on the first Sabbath after the removal of Mr Pitchtone. They went, indeed, at a very early hour, for the purpose of avoiding notice, and took their seats in some unappropriated pews in a very distant, and almost invisible quarter of the gallery.

The entire congregation having assembled, the clergyman waited some time for the accustomed appearance of the sons and daughters of sacred song. It is almost universally the practice throughout our New England country churches, to commence public worship with the singing of a psalm or hymn. On the present occasion, no person being ostensibly ready to perform that duty, the minister began the services with the 'long prayer.' Yet, when this was concluded, an imperious necessity occurred, of making at least the attempt to diversify and animate the business of the sanctuary, by an act of melody. Accordingly the Rev. Mr Welby announced and read the psalm adapted to the subject of the sermon which was to succeed. Then, having waited a moment or two, during which a most painful silence and suspense pervaded the congregation, he began, in a voice naturally strong and clear, to sing the psalm alone, still keeping his usual standing position in the centre of the pulpit Only one voice was heard to support him. It was that of the venerable deacon, who sat immediately beneath, and who hummed a broken kind of bass, without the accompaniment of words, there being scarcely a hymn book in the lower part of the meetinghouse. The same scene occurred in the afternoon, with the slight addition of a female voice in some part of the house, which lent its modest, unskilful, and half-suppressed assistance through the concluding portion of the hymn.

Matters went on nearly in this way for the space of a month, at the end of which, the singing began to improve a little, by the gradual return to church, though not to the singing gallery, of the stragglers who had composed the late choir, and who were now willing to join in the vocal duties of worship under the auspices of the pastor. At length, when about six months had been thus dragged along, an occasion offered for a return to the deserted orchestra, in a manner which might somewhat shelter the mortification and inspire the confidence of the rallied choristers.

A Mr Ebed Harrington, who had recently removed into the village for the purpose of studying medicine with the physician of the place, had some pretensions on the musical score. He was an unmarried man, of about the age of thirty years, and had been, until this period, a hard-working labourer on his father's farm, which was situated in an obscure township in New Hampshire. His complexion was of the darkest, his face exactly circular, his eyes small, black, and unmeaning, his form thickset, and the joints of his principal limbs had been contracted by nature or use into inflexible angles of considerable acuteness. He defrayed the expenses of his board and medical tuition by labouring agriculturally the half of every day, for his teacher, Dr Saddlebags. The other half of the day, and a large portion of the night, were industriously devoted by our incipient Esculapius to the study of his new-chosen profession, with the exception of a few evenings which he occasionally spent at different places in the neighborhood. It was on one of these visits that he found means to exhibit some imposing specimens of his abilities in the performance of sacred music. And having suggested that he had often taken the lead in the choir of his native parish, he almost immediately received a pressing invitation from some of the most active of the singers in Waterfield, to place himself at their head, on the following Sabbath, and thus enable them to supply the lamented vacancy, which existed in the apparatus of worship at their meetinghouse.

The invitation was accepted. That quarter of the singing seats devoted to the female sex, was filled at an early hour on the next Sabbath morning, by fair occupants, furnished generally each with her hymn book, and waiting with some impatience for the other moiety of the choir to arrive, and for the services to begin. The body of male performers gradually assembled at one corner of the building, out of doors, and discussed several particulars relating to the important movement which was now about to take place. One difficulty that staggered the most of them, was, the manner in which Mr Ebed Harrington, their new precentor, should be introduced into the singing gallery. He himself, modestly suggested the propriety of being conducted by some one of the gentlemen singers to the spot. But besides that there was not an individual in the circle who conceived himself clothed with sufficient authority, or who felt sufficient confidence in himself, to enact so grave a ceremony, it appeared to be the general opinion, that Mr Harrington, in virtue of his newly conferred office, should march into church at the head of the choir. While they were debating this point with no little earnestness, the time was

sliding rapidly away. All the rest of the
congregation, even to the last tardy strag-
gler, had entered and taken their seats. An
impatient and wondering stillness mantled
over the whole assemblage within, and Mr
Welby was on the point of rising to an-
nounce the psalm, at the hazard of whatever
consequences might ensue, when, by a sud-
den, spontaneous, and panic-like movement,
which I cannot remember who of us began,
the tuneful collection without, suspended
their debate, and rushed in a body into the
front door of the meetinghouse. Part of us
turned off immediately into the right aisle,
and part into the left. The stairs leading to
the gallery were placed at the end of each
of these aisles, at two corners of the building
within, so that whoever mounted them was
exposed to the view of the congregation.
With a hurried and most earnest solemnity,
the choristers made their trampling way up
these stairs, and soon found themselves in a
large octagonal pew in the centre of the
front gallery. Each individual occupied the

seat which he could first reach, and Mr
Harrington, without being offered the post
of honour usually assigned the leader, was
fain, in the general confusion and forgetful-
ness of the scene, to assume about four in-
ches of the edge of a bench contiguous to
the door of the pew. Here, while wiping
from his brow, with a red dotted calico
handkerchief, the perspiration which the
anxieties and exertions of the moment had
profusely excited, the voice of the clergyman
in the pulpit restored him and his fellow
singers to the calm of recollection, and fixed all eyes around upon him as their legiti-
mate guide.

The tune which he selected was well
adapted to the hymn announced. Every
body remembers Wells. Mr Harrington
had forgotten to take a pitchpipe with him to
the place of worship, and there was accident-
ally no instrument of any kind present. He
was therefore obliged to trust to his ear or
rather to his fortune for the pitch of the
leading note. The fourth note in the tune

of Wells happens to be an octave above the first. Unluckily, Mr Harrington seized upon a pitch better adapted to this fourth note than to the first. The consequence was, that in leading off the tune, to the words of ' Life is the time,' he executed the three first notes with considerable correctness, though with not a little straining, but in attempting to pronounce the word *time*, he found that nature had failed to accommodate his voice with a sound sufficiently high for the purpose. The rest of the tenor voices were surprised into the same consciousness. Here then he was brought to an absolute stand, and with him, the whole choir, with the exception of two or three of the most ardent singers of the bass and treble, whose enthusiasm and earnestness carried them forward nearly through the first line, before they perceived the calamity which had befallen their head-quarters. They now reluctantly suffered their voices one after another to drop away, and a dead silence of a moment ensued. Mr Harrington began

again, with a somewhat lower pitch of voice,
and with stepping his feet a little back, as if
to leap forward to some imaginary point; but
still with no greater success. A similar
catastrophe to the former, awaited this second attempt. The true sound for the word
time, still remained far beyond the utmost
reach of his falsetto. In his third effort, he
was more fortunate, since he hit upon a
leading note, which brought the execution
of the whole tune just within the compass of
possibility, and the entire six verses were
discussed with much spirit and harmony.
When the hymn was finished, the leader and
several of his more intimate acquaintances
exchanged nods and smiles with each other,
compounded of mortification and triumph—
mortification at the mistakes with which the
singing had begun, and triumph at the spirited manner in which it was carried on and
concluded. This foolish and wicked practice is indulged in too many choirs, by some
of the leading singers, who ought to set a
better example to their fellow choristers, and

compose themselves into other than giggling and winking frames of mind, at the moment when a whole congregation are about to rise or kneel in a solemn act of praise and prayer.

The greater part of the interval between the first and second singing, which was occupied by the minister and the devout portion of his hearers in a high and solemn communion with the Deity, was devoted by Mr Harrington and his associates above-mentioned, to turning over the leaves of the Village Harmony, and making a conditional choice of the tune next to be performed, according to the metre of the hymn which might be read. When the time arrived for their second performance, although Mr Harrington was more happy than before, in catching the true key-note of the air, yet, either from some deficiency of science in himself, or from a misapprehension on the part of those who sang bass, this important department of the choir began the hymn with a note which happened to be the most discordant of the whole scale. The consequence was dreadful to every one within hearing, who was afflicted with a good ear. Our Coryphæus interposed his authority to produce silence, by emitting through his teeth a loud and protracted hush ! After some little difficulty, they succeeded in starting fairly, and carried on the performance with due harmony of tones.

In the afternoon, Mr Harrington was at his post as settled leader of the choir. It is true that he found himself surrounded by only about half the number of assistants who had attended the commencement of his vocal career in the morning. But no one had ventured to insinuate to him his incompetency, and several of the singers charitably ascribed his mistakes to the accidental absence of the pitchpipe, and to the modest trepidation which naturally arose from his first appearance. His principal mistake on the latter part of the day, was that of selecting a common metre tune which ought to have been one in long metre. He perceiv-

ed not his error, until he arrived at the end
of the second line, when, finding that he had
yet two more syllables to render into music,
he at first attempted to eke out the air by a
kind of flourish of his own, in a suppressed
and hesitating voice. But he was soon
convinced that this would never do. Had
he been entirely alone, he might in this way
have carried the hymn through, trusting to
his own musical resources and invention.
But it was out of his power to inspire the
other singers with the foreknowledge of the
exact notes which his genius might devise
and append to every second line. They,
too, must try their skill to the same purpose,
and while the whole choir, tenor, bass, and
treble, were each endeavoring to eke out the
line with their own efforts and happy flour-
ishes, a tremendous clash of discord and
chaos of uncertainty involved both the leaders and the led together. There was nothing in this dilemma, therefore, for him to do,
except to stop short at once, and select a
new tune. This he did with much prompt-

ness and apparent composure, though, that there was some little flutter in his bosom, was evident from the circumstance that the tune he again pitched upon, contrary to all rules in the course of a single Sabbath, was Wells,—which, however, went off with much propriety, and with none of the interruptions that had marred its performance in the morning.

There are many of the thorough-bred sons of New England, whose perseverance it takes much greater discouragements to daunt than befel the precentorial efforts of Mr Ebed Harrington on this memorable day. He regarded himself now as the fully instated leader of the choir in Waterfield ; a function which he inflexibly maintained, through good report and through evil report, sometimes amidst almost entire desertion, and at other times with a very respectable band to follow his guidance—until his professional studies were completed, and he himself removed from the neighbourhood, to plunge into some of the newly settled territories for an establishment,

and introduce, perchance, the arts of healing
and melody together. I have never heard
one word of his destination or subsequent
success.

The musical concerns of our parish were
not involved in the same embarrassment after
his departure, as after that of his predecessor. Young Williams had now increased in
years, skill, and confidence. Nature had
destined him to be a passionate votary of
music. He was scarcely out of mere boy-
hood, before he grasped the violoncello—or,
as we term it in New England, the bass-viol—
with a kind of preternatural adroitness, and
clung to it with a devoted and ardent perseverance, which very soon rendered him an
accomplished performer. Every leisure hour,
every leisure moment he could seize, was
employed on this his favorite instrument.
The first ray of morning was welcomed by
the vibrations of its Memnonian strings.
Many a meal was cheerfully foregone, that
he might feed his ear and his soul with the
more ethereal food to which his desires tend-

ed. Often too were his musical exercises
protracted far beyond midnight, to the annoyance at first of his father's family, who soon
however, could sleep as well beneath the
sounds of the lad's violoncello, as if an Æolian
harp were soothingly ringing all night at their
windows. As he sat in the solitude of his
chamber, a solitude sweetened by his own
exquisite skill and the indulgence of his fond
taste, he regarded not the cold of winter and
not always the darkness of the night. He
speedily made himself master of his darling
science, as far as such an attainment was
possible from the introductions to all the com-
pilations of music within his reach, from
Dobson's Encyclopedia,* and from such
other appropriate books as the Waterfield
Social Library and Mr Welby's humble collection of miscellaneous literature might supply. His performance was the admiration
of all the country round. His father's house
was frequently visited for the single purpose

* Dobson reprinted in Philadelphia the Encyclopedia
Britannica, referred to in the text.

of witnessing the display of his uncommon talents. Most willingly did he exhibit his powers before the representative to Congress, or Mr Welby and his family, or a bevy of admiring girls, or a half dozen ragged children, who were attracted from their plays in the streets and the fields, to be soothed and charmed and civilized into silence by our self-taught Orpheus. Now, he would draw tears from every eye by the tremulous and complaining pathos of the string as he wound through some mournful air. Now he would make every soul burn, and every cheek glow with lofty rapture as he executed the splendid movements of Washington's March, Belle-isle March, Hail Columbia, or the much less admirable, but equally popular Ode to Science. Now, by a seemingly miraculous rapidity and perfection of execution, he would exert an irresistible power over the muscular frames of his delighted auditors, putting their feet and hands in motion as they sat before him, and often rousing up the younger individuals who were present to an unbidden, spontaneous dance, to the tune of 'The Girl I left behind me,' the 'Devil's Dream,' or an equally magical and inspiring combination of notes that extemporaneously flowed into his own mind on the occasion. During all these scenes, his own fair countenance was rarely ever observed to alter in the least from a certain composed, though elevated and steadfast abstraction. Occasionally, however, the occurrence of a plaintive strain would throw a kind of compassionate softness into his looks, and some sublime movement of melody or new combination of harmony would fill his rolling eye with tears. The motion of his arm and the posture of his body were indescribably graceful. To some persons of extravagant fancy, he seemed, while playing upon his noble instrument, to be sitting on a cloud, that was wafting him about in the atmosphere of sounds which he created. Sometimes the viol and the bow appeared to be portions of himself, which he handled with the same dexterity that nature teaches the soul to exert over its own body. Sometimes

again you would imagine him in love with the
instrument, as if he had no other mistress in
the world to fix his serious and impassioned
looks upon, and be agitated by her enchant-
ments. For several minutes he would lay
his ear down near the strings, and then
throw his body far back, and his eye upward,
while, in this new position, his head kept
time with a gentle motion, and with a sort
of unconcious ease. He never refused to
play the most common or indifferent air ; a
circumstance, that resulted partly from his
good nature, which would not suffer him to
be fastidious or disobliging, and partly from
his own concious ability to make music out
of a tune, which of itself had small pretensions. Indeed he was one of those few performers, who array in a new and peculiar
dress every piece which they attempt to ex-
ecute. Written notes before him were but
a skeleton, which he not merely clothed with
a body and animated with a life, but into
which he infused a soul and an inspiration
that none but the rarest geniuses on earth
can cause to exist.

Such was the temporary successor to Mr,
or now, more properly speaking, Dr Ebed
Harrington in the government of the sacred
choir at Waterfield. Charles Williams, as
I have before observed, was as yet too
young to take the lead in the melodious department of public worship, when that interesting and uncouth personage came to reside
in the village. But it is very questionable
whether the pretensions of the latter to his
honorable office in the gallery would ever
have been submitted to during the two years
that he remained, had he been destitute of
the assistance rendered him by the musical
young Crispin whom I have just introduced to
my readers. Charles had been almost constantly at his post as leader of the bass, and
performer on the violoncello. Sometimes,
indeed, on a fine Sunday morning, late in
May, or perhaps in midsummer, or early in
October, he would take his instrument, and
steal alone and unperceived to some retreat
about two miles from the village. Here our
truant genius would seat himself beneath an

oak, and try the effect of mingling the audible sounds of his viol with the *felt* harmony of sunshine, breeze, and shade ; interrupting for a moment or two the chirp of the squirrel and the Greek talk * of the blackbird, but then again stimulating them to a more violent little concert in company with his own instrument, and the long ringing note of the grasshopper, as it hung suspended and motionless over the ground, amidst the calm glare of a burning sun. The delicious enjoyment afforded him by such occasions as these would have tempted him to very frequent indulgences of the kind, had not the music in the meetinghouse suffered so much from his absence, and had he not been aware that such conduct was the cause of considerable uneasiness and half-reproachful regret among a

---

* What schoolboy has not listened with delighted astonishment to the almost exact conjugation of something like a Greek verb, which the blackbird gives him in its Πολλω, πολω, πεπληκα ? Which of the winged tribe has a better itle to Mr Gray's compliment of ' Attic warbler ? '

large portion of the congregation. Blessed influence of Christian institutions, and of the severe forms of social life, that check the movements of selfishness and eccentricity, and recal the thoughtless wanderer back to the course of duty ! Who can complain at the comparatively slight sacrifices which they enjoin, and at the contribution to the common stock of happiness which they demand, in return for the protection, the field of exertion, the inexhaustible sources of enjoyment, and the paths to the attainment of every species of individual excellence which they so abundantly furnish ?

On the elevation of Charles Williams to the seat of leader of the choir, new life was infused into the whole vocal company. Years had done something for him since the period at which our history commences, but experience and the opening native energy of his mind had done much more. Implicit confidence was now reposed in his skill and management even by the shyest member of the choir. He had occasionally supplied the

accidental absence of Mr Harrington, and
had been constantly consulted by that gen-
man with peculiar deference in all the business, and mystery, and apparatus, incident
to the due administration of his office. It
was even whispered round in the singing
pews, that Charles had often been happily
instrumental in correcting or preventing several blunders on the part of his superior, not
unlike those which I before recorded as dis-
tinguishing the outset of that gentleman's
career.

With such qualifications, and such a reputation, Mr Williams entered upon his dig-
nities with the highest spirit and the best
prospects of success. The choir was in-
stantly replenished by all the old deserters
and by many new recruits. Singing meet-
ings were appointed in private houses on
two or three evenings of each week for the
purpose of practice and improvement. A
large supply of the (then) last edition of the
Village Harmony was procured, and the
stock of good pieces, which all might famil-

iarly sing, was enlarged. The whole number of performers was about fifty. This was one of those happy and brilliant periods which all our New England churches occasionally enjoy for a longer or shorter term in the musical department of the sacred exercises. I will not contend that the psalms now went off with much science or expression. Charles Williams was fully equal to the task of infusing the best possible taste in these respects into the choir which he led. But he wisely felt that his authority did not extend quite so far at present as to warrant the attempt to introduce among them any nice innovations on the oldfashioned manner of vocal performance. He was not their teacher in the art. He was only one of themselves, and all he could expect to do, was to yield himself to the general stream of musical taste and prejudice, with the exception of such little improvements as he hoped to effect by his sole example, or the communication of his ideas in private to some particular friends. He accordingly

began and executed the most galloping fugues and the most unexpressive airs with the
same spirit and alacrity that he would have
expended on the divinest strains of sacred
music.

Notwithstanding, however, these slight
unavoidable deficiencies, the present was,
as I observed, a bright and happy period in
the meetinghouse at Waterfield. There was
a full choir. It was punctual in its attendance at church. The singing, though a little noisy, was at least generally correct in
time and tone. A new anthem was gotten
up at the recurrence of each Fast and
Thanksgiving Day, and funeral anthems were
sung on the Sabbath that immediatly succeeded any interment in the parish. There
are few who will not acknowledge the luxury
of such a state of things, when compared
with the necessity of enduring, Sabbath after
Sabbath, a feeble, poor, discordant band of
singers, or listening to the performance of
two or three scattered individuals among the
congregation, who go through their duty with

reluctance, and seem not so much to be singing praises, as offering up substitutes and
apologies.

Far different from such a picture were the
achievements of our renovated choir. Every
tune which they performed seemed to be a
triumph over the preceding. Charles Williams was so much in his element that he inspired all around him with the same feeling.

It is true, there were some peculiarities
in the manners and customs of the choir, to
which a fastidious stranger might object. In
warm weather, Charles assumed the liberty
of laying aside his coat, and exhibiting the
perfection to which his sisters could bleach
his linen, in which practice he was supported by about half the men-singers present.
Another exceptionable habit prevailed among
us. As soon as the hymn was read, and
those ominous preluding notes distributed
round, which come before the performance
of a psalm-tune like scattering drops before
a shower, that portion of the band, which
sat in front of the gallery, suddenly arose,

wheeled their backs round to the audience
below, and commenced operations with all
possible earnestness and ardour. Thus the
only part of the congregation which they
faced, consisted of those, who sat in the
range of pews, that ran along behind the
singing seats.

It was somewhat unnecessary, moreover,
that each individual performer should beat
time on his own account. But this was a
habit of inveterate standing in the church,
which nothing short of the omnipotent voice
of fashion could be hoped to frighten away.
That voice was not yet heard to this effect
in the singing gallery at Waterfield. But it
would have cost many an occupant there a
pang to resign the privilege of this little display. Let Mr D'Israeli and the editor of
Blackwood's Magazine inspect the disposi-
tions of men in their hand-writing. But as
a school for the study of character, give *me*
a choir of singers, who are in the habit of
beating time, each for himself. How could
the most superficial observer mistake these

characteristic symptoms? Here and there
you might see a hand ostentatiously and un-
shrinkingly lifted above all surrounding heads
like the sublime and regular recurrence of a
windmill's wings. Some performers there
were, who studied an inexpressible and inim-
itable grace in every modification of motion
to which they subjected their finger-joints,
wrists, elbows, shoulders, and bodies. Some
tossed the limb up and down with an energy that seemed to be resenting an affront.
Others were so gentle in their vibrations,
that they appeared afraid of disturbing the
serenity of the circumambient air. Some
hands swept a full segment of one hundred
and eighty degrees; others scarcely advanced farther than the minute-hand of a
stop-watch at a single pulsation. The young
student at law, the merchant's clerk, and a
few others, whom fortune had exempted from
the primeval malediction of personal toil,
were at once recognised by the easy freedom with which they waved a hand that no
sun had browned and the contact of no ag-

ricultural implement had roughened. If, as we have seen, some of the singers were ostentatious in wielding an arm to its full extent, others were equally ostentatious in using only a finger, or a thumb and middle finger joined. To the honor of the choir, however, be it said, that there were several of its members, who performed the duty, which was then customary, of beating time, without any effort or affectation. It should also be ascribed to nothing more than a sense of propriety and laudable modesty, that a great part of the female singers kept time in no other way than by moving a forefinger which hung down at their sides, and was almost concealed amidst large folds of changeable silk, or of glazed colored cotton cambric. To this a few of them added a slight motion of the head or body, while some of the married ladies openly raised and lowered their hands upon the hymn books from which they sang.

In addition to the foregoing general imperfections, which prevented the congregation at Waterfield from witnessing the *beau ideal* of a sacred choir, it is to be lamented that there were others, which resulted not from common custom, but from individual peculiarities. The taste and knowledge of music, among all the performers, were far from being uniform. While some sang with great beauty of expression, and a nice adjustment to the sentiment of the happy modulations of a flexible voice, others made no more distinction between the different notes than did the printed singing book itself, or any lifeless instrument that gives out the tone required with the same strength and the same unvaried uniformity on all occasions. Nothing, too, could be rougher than the Stentorian voice of Mr Broadbreast, and nothing more piercing than the continued shriek of the pale but enthusiastic Miss Sixfoot. I shall not disclose the name of the good man who annoyed us a little with his ultra-nasal twang; nor of another, who, whenever he took the true pitch, did so by a happy accident ; nor of another, who had an ungainly trick of catching his breath violently at every third note ; nor of several of both sexes, whose pronunciation of many words, particularly of *how*, *now*, &c. was dreadfully rustic, and hardly to be expressed on paper. Jonathan Oxgoad sang indeed much too loud, but that could have been forgiven him, had he not perpetually forgotten what verses were directed by the minister to be omitted ; a neglect, which, before he discovered his error, often led him half through an interdicted verse, much to the annoyance of the worthy pastor, the confusion of his fellow singers, the vexation of the congregation, and the amusement and gratification of Jonathan's too goodnatured friends.

There was also a culpable neglect among the male singers in providing themselves with a sufficient number of hymn books. That it was not so on the other side of the choir, was partly owing to the delicate tact of women, which never suffers them to violate even the minor proprieties of time and place, and partly to their greater attachment to religion. As, in our New England churches, generally, we have no prayer books to serve as a kind of endearing bond between the public and domestic altar, the vivid imagination and tender affection of the female singer caused her to cherish her hymn book in such a connexion. The more rough, careless, and indifferent habits of our own sex render us less attentive to these sensible memorials for the heart. Accordingly, in our choir, among the men, the proportion of books was scarcely more than one to four or five performers, so that you might often hear some ardent and confident individual, who was stationed too far from the page to read distinctly, attempting to make out the sentence from his own imagination,—or, when he despaired of achieving that aim, filling up the line with uncouth and unheard-of syllables, or with inarticulate sounds. It is strange how some little inconveniences of this kind will be borne for a long time without an effort made for their remedy. It was not avarice which caused this deficiency of

hymn books ; far from it ; it was only the
endurance of an old custom, which it occurred to no one to take the proper steps to
remove. Was it not thirty years that uncle
Toby threatened every day to oil the creaking hinge that gave him so much anguish of
soul—and threatened in vain ?

But I will no longer contemplate the sha-
dy points of my picture. On the whole, the
blemishes just described, were scarce ever
offensively perceptible, when compared with
the general merit with which the singing
was conducted and continued to improve for
the space of two or three years. Besides,
our supply of good music was equal or superior to the demand. Be it remembered, that
we were singing within wooden walls to the
edification of an American country congregation, who sprang unmixed from Puritanical
ancestors, and not beneath the dome of an
European metropolitan cathedral.

It is impossible to look back without some
of the animation of triumph upon those
golden hours of my early manhood, when I

stood among friends and acquaintances, and
we all started off with the keenest alacrity
in some favorite air, that made the roof of
our native church resound, and caused the
distant, though unfrequent traveller to pause
upon his way, for the purpose of more distinctly catching the swelling and dying
sounds that waved over the hills and rever-
berated from wood to wood.   The grand and
rolling bass of Charles Williams's viol, beneath which the very floor was felt to trem-
ble, was surmounted by the strong, rich, and
exquisite tenor of his own matchless voice.
And oh ! at the turning of a fugue, when the
bass moved forward first, like the opening
fire of artillery, and the tenor advanced next
like a corps of grenadiers, and the treble
followed on with the brilliant execution of
infantry, and the trumpet counter shot by
the whole, with the speed of darting cavalry,
and then, when we all mingled in that battle
of harmony and melody, and mysteriously
fought our way through each verse with a
well ordered perplexity, that made the

audience wonder how we ever came out
exactly together, (which once in a while,
indeed, owing to some strange surprise or
lingering among the treble, we failed to do,)
the sensations that agitated me at those
moments, have rarely been equalled during
the monotonous pilgrimage of my life.

And yet, when I remember how little we
kept in view the main and real object of
sacred music—when I think how much we
sang to the praise and honor and glory of
our inflated selves alone—when I reflect
that the majority of us absolutely did not
intend that any other ear in the universe
should listen to our performances, save those
of the admiring human audience below and
around us—I am inclined to feel more shame
and regret than pleasure at these youthful
recollections, and must now be permitted to
indulge for a few pages in a more serious
strain.

How large and dreadful is the account
against numberless ostensible Christian worshippers in this respect ! And how decisive

might be the triumph of the Roman Catholics over Protestants, if they chose to urge it in this quarter ! They might demand of us, what we have gained by greater simplicity and abstractness of forms. They might ask, whether it is not equally abominable in the sight of Jehovah, that music should be abused in his sanctuary, as that pictures and images should be perverted from their original design ? For my part, I conscientiously think that there is more piety, more of the spirit of true religion, in the idolatry which kneels in mistaken, though heartfelt gratitude to a sculptured image, than in the deliberate mockery which sends up solemn sounds from thoughtless tongues. How often does what is called sacred music, administer only to the vanity of the performer and the gratification of the hearer, who thus, as it were, themselves inhale the incense which they are solemnly wafting, though they have full enough need that it should ascend and find favour for them with the Searcher of all Hearts !

This is a rock of temptation which the Quakers have avoided; in dispensing with the inspiration of song, they at least shun its abuses; and if they really succeed in filling their hour with intense religious meditation and spiritual communion—if, from their still retreat, the waves of this boisterous world are excluded, and send thither no disturbing ripple—if no calculations of interest, and no sanguine plans are there prosecuted, and no hopes, nor fears, nor regrets, nor triumphs, nor recollections, nor any other flowers that grow this side of the grave, are gathered and pressed to the bosom, on the margin of those quiet waters—if, in short, the very silence and vacancy of the scene are not too much for the feeble heart of man, which, if deprived of the stay of external things, will either fall back on itself, or else will rove to the world's end to expend its restless activity in a field of chaotic imaginations;—if, I say, the Quakers are so happy as to escape these perils, together with the seductions to vanity and self-gratification

which music and preaching present, then
must their worship, I think, be the purest of
all worship, and their absence of exterior
forms the very perfection of all forms.   But,
let me ask of thee, my heart, whether *thou*
couldst fulfil the above severe conditions ?
Wouldst thou no longer obtrusively beat and
ache beneath the external serenity of a
Quaker's composed demeanour and unmodish
apparel, and voiceless celebration ?   Thou
shrinkest from the trial, and art still convinced that the road in which thou canst best
be trained for Heaven, lies somewhere at an
equal distance between the bewildering mag-
nificence of the Romish ritual, and the bar-
ren simplicity of silent worship.

I have long doubted whether, in the prevailing musical customs among our New
England Independent churches, there be not
something more unfavorable to the cause
and progress of pure devotion, than can be
charged against many other popular denomi-
nations.   The Methodist, and the strict
Presbyterian, have no separate choirs.   They

have not yet succeeded so far in the division
of spiritual labour, as to delegate to others
the business of praise, or to worship God by
proxy. I have often witnessed a congregation of one thousand Methodists, as they rose
simultaneously from their seats, and following the officiating minister, who gave out
the hymn in portions of two lines, joined all
together in some simple air, which expressed the very soul of natural music. I could
see no lips closed as far as I could direct
my vision, nor could I hear one note of discord uttered. Was it that the heartiness
and earnestness which animated the whole
throng, inspired even each tuneless individual with powers not usually his own, and
sympathetically dragged into the general
stream of harmony, those voices which were
not guided by a musical ear ? or was it, that
the overwhelming majority of good voices,
such as, I presume, if exerted, would prevail in every congregation, drowned the im
perfect tones, and the occasional inaccura-
cies of execution, which most probably ex-

isted ? It did not offend me that they sang
with all their might, and all their soul, and
all their strength ; for it was evident that
they sang with all their heart. I was conscious of hearing only one grand and rolling
volume of sound, which swallowed up minor
asperities and individual peculiarities. This
was particularly the case after two or three
verses were sung, when the congregation
had been wrought into a kind of movement
of inspiration. Then the strains came to
my ear with the sublimity of a rushing
mighty torrent, and with an added beauty
of melody that the waters cannot give.
The language was still distinctly intelli-
gible, and the time perfectly preserved.
And although, when I retired from the scene,
I could not say how expressively this chorister had sung, nor how exquisitely the other
had trilled, nor could compliment a single
lady on her golden tones, nor criticise the
fine science of the counterpoint, yet I felt
that I had been thrilled and affected in a
better way, and could not but wish that what

was really to be approved of among the Methodists, might be imitated in those happier churches, where religion is cultivated without protracting her orgies into midnight, and cordially embraced without the necessity of delirious screams, and apoplectic swoons.

Perhaps it may be thought that the good old Presbyterian way of accompanying a clerk, or precentor, who is stationed beneath the pulpit, in front of the congregation, will most generally secure the true spirit and perfection of sacred music. Born and nurtured an Independent as I am, I confess that I sometimes feel inclined to the adoption of this opinion, with a few additions and modifications. There is certainly an advantage in imposing upon a single individual the business of leading the melodious part of public devotion. It must necessarily constrain the congregation to unite their voices with his, unless they are totally lost to all sense of the proprieties of the sanctuary. This custom, moreover, must exclude those miserable feuds and other sources of interruption, which will always to a greater or less degree disturb a separately constituted choir.

But in conceding thus much to the children of the Westminster Assembly, I would beg leave to be strenuous in insisting upon a recommendation that may appear very strange as coming from a disciple of John Robinson. I cannot find it in my soul to dispense with the glorious majesty of sound with which an organ fills the house of prayer. In the tones of this sublime trophy of human skill, there is something that wondrously accords with the sentiment of piety. We know that martial bravery, love, joy, and other feelings of our nature, have each their peculiar and stirring instruments of sound. The connexion between religion and the organ, too, is something more than fanciful. Who has not felt at once inspired and subdued by the voice issuing from that gilded little sanctuary, which towers in architectural elegance over the solemn assembly below, and seems to enshrine the presiding genius of devotional praise ?

I am aware that even the united aid of a precentor and organ are insufficient to check certain tendencies to the decline of good singing, which may insidiously creep into a whole musical congregation with the lapse of time. Tunes, it may be said, grow old, and weary the ear ; wretched voices may prevail over the better sort ; in one pew, a worshipper may always sing the tenor part in a voice of the deepest bass ; in another pew, every psalm may be screamed through with one whole note out of the way ; a devotion like that of the Methodists, which often seems to make them sing decently in spite of themselves, must not be expected to continue long ; a fashion of indifference towards this department of worship may arise and prevail ; and especially, the extensive cultivation of secular music in private families may render very many ears so fastidious, as absolutely to frustrate the object of sacred music at church, since the tasteless and indiscriminate clamour necessarily produced by the voices of a mixed congregation, must tend to excite in the more refined classes a disgusted and indevout spirit, rather than the sweet and lofty aspirations of choral praise. On all these accounts, it may possibly be argued, that our later ancestors have done well in withdrawing from the general congregation the performance of this service, and assigning it to a select choir, who, by concentrating their efforts, and reducing the matter to something of a profession, may keep the stream of sacred song at least pure, though small.

Nearly all the above sinister tendencies, however, might, I apprehend, be counteracted by the application of a little care and system. To prevent the repetition of old tunes from palling on the ear, a new one might occasionally be introduced by the clerk, and sung every Sabbath until the congregation were familiar with it. The affliction caused by bad voices might be disposed of by the appointment of a musical censor, or standing committee, whose duty it should be, to exercise now and then an act of delicate au-

thority, acquainting the well-meaning offend-
ers with the fact of their vocal disability, and
requesting from them in future an edifying
silence. As to the decay of devotion, and
the increase of indifference among a congregation, these appear to me to be far from
good reasons for establishing a separate
choir, and are rather proofs that such a choir
will effect no sort of good. With respect to
the last evil which a select choir is supposed to avoid, the fastidiousness occasioned by
the private and profane cultivation of musical taste, I know not why a whole congregation, or at least all the efficient voices in it,
may not be systematically taught good church
music, and the best and purest taste be made
general among them.

But I will candidly allow that some of
these schemes of improvement are rather
visionary than practical. Sitting at home in
one's office, one can easily devise remedies
for existing social defects, but in attempting
to put them into execution, the science of
human nature is found to be ten times more

embarrassing than hydrostatics itself. Some obstinate pressure from an unsuspected quarter may burst over the feeble mounds which we are fondly erecting about an imaginary reservoir of beauty and tranquillity. It is a very enchanting employment of the mind to draw sketches of a kind of abstract congregation, where every one present joins in the prayer, and listens profitably to the sermon, and keeps constantly awake, and takes devout part in the psalmody, and where no eye is suffered to wander, nor attention to flag, nor worldly dreams to intrude. But where is there such a congregation on earth ? And would even a Handel succeed in tutoring a mixed audience into a celestial choir of angels ? On these accounts, I am not disposed to push my censures or my native communion too far. Perhaps novelty and imagination have done a little in recommending to me the practices of other churches, and if I were familiar with the whole history of their musical condition, I might tell as many strange stories of them, as I

am rehearsing of my own. I am not sufficiently read in Puritanical antiquarianism
to know whether the Independents once re-
sembled the Presbyterians in the mode of
conducting sacred music, and afterwards
found it necessary in the course of time to
institute distinct choirs, or whether they on
purpose instituted a custom diametrically
opposite to that of their rival sectaries, after
the fashion in which these last had themselves
abolished surplices and organs. Neal is silent on these curious points. If one may
judge from some merry traditions prevalent
in New England, our good forefathers had
no choirs, but sang under the dictation of
one and sometimes two lines at a time from
the minister or a clerk. Most of us have
heard of singular divisions to which poor
Sternhold and Hopkins were subjected by
this custom. Thus,

> "The Lord will come, and he will not
> Keep silence, but speak out,"

used to make perplexing sense to the pil-
grims, when given out to them by a line at

a time ; for that such was the manner of
uttering it, I have understood from a clergyman who learned it at a Massachusetts Con-
vention dinner twenty years ago, where the
agreeable and Orthodox Dr——set the
table in a roar by relating the anecdote.—
It is probable, then, that experience and necessity in the lapse of time have forced upon
our congregations the present universal custom of assigning to a few individuals the task
of leading the praises in public worship.   It
might now be dangerous, or rather impracti-
ble, to introduce a reformation.   If imperfections exist, perhaps they are a choice of
the least.   Yet still it were to be wished
that the choir might not be regarded, so
much as it is, the sole medium through
which this portion of worship is offered.   It
were to be wished that our audiences would
consider that body as leaders only, not performers ; to be followed and accompanied,
not to be listened to for luxurious gratification, or fastidious criticism, or as an eked
out variety of the tedious business of a Sun-

day. I can conceive that a choir, if properly instituted and administered, might be exceedingly useful in extending and preserving a true tone of taste, in keeping up a good selection of sacred music, and in acting, so to speak, as the teachers of the congregation, in these and kindred respects. But in the very duty thus prescribed them lies their deplorable danger and temptation. They are unavoidably liable, as was above intimated, to resolve the matter into a mere profession. In the study of sacred music as a science, and the cultivation of it as an art, they forget its ultimate object. Nor could much else be expected from the narrowness of the human mind. Must it not be hard to attend to the thousand little circumstances which a skilful performance requires, and at the same time to keep the heart strained up to a pitch of due devotion? And on the supposition that by practice and habit we can acquire a perfect familiarity with the pieces to be performed, and a mutual confidence can be obtained among all the members of the choir ; yet, alas, it is in the very process of cultivating this practice and habit, that the spirit of devotion is apt to evaporate, and to leave us admirable performers rather than cordial worshippers.

This state of things, moreover, has its temptations for the audience at large. The more beautiful the music, the greater is their inclination to listen and admire, rather than to bear a part. It seems a kind of sacrilege to let my indifferent voice break in upon the divine strains which are charming my ear. But the real sacrilege is in my refraining from the duty. Probably, about the most perfect and affecting sacred music in this country is that at the Andover Theological Seminary. Yet who, in listening to the exquisite anthem sung at the anniversary of that institution, does not find himself unconsciously betrayed into an earthly ecstacy of weeping admiration, in which, on analysis, he is surprised and ashamed to find that mere religion has but little, if any share ?

Such always have been and always will be the dangers resulting from the conversion of taste and the arts into handmaids of religion. Perpetual efforts are requisite to keep them from becoming her mistresses at last. I appeal to the consciences of hundreds of congregations, who are in the habit of sitting, Sabbath after Sabbath, with Epicurean complacency, and silently listening to the music above them, as to a gratuitous and pleasant entertainment. I appeal with more confidence to the consciences of a thousand choirs, who are engrossed in the anxious business of carrying a psalm off well, and are distracted with numerous likings and antipathies about different tunes, whether they do not commonly feel cut off, as by a kind of professional fence, from the devotional sympathies and sacred engagements of the congregation in general. Sharing no active or conspicuous part in the other services, but so very active and conspicuous a part in *one*, is it not the case, that they take little, if any interest in the former, and regard them rather in the light of a foil to set off their own paramount achievements, than as a votive wreath, into which it is their privilege, duty, and felicity, to weave an humble flower ?

Sorry I am to acknowledge that such were the predominant feelings in the choir at Waterfield at that point of time in its history from which I have been led insensibly so far away by a dull train of digressive reflections. It is impossible to say how much of this defective sentiment may have been owing to the circumstance of our leader being a gay and rather inconsiderate young man, whom the whole of us were constrained to admire for his musical excellence and many parts of his private character. Certain it is, that Charles Williams had no other holier aspiration or thought at that time than to acquit himself with applause as the chief of a vocal company. In every other respect, his example would scarcely be recommended on the score of seriousness or piety. A little knot of whisperers was often gathered round him during both the prayer and the delivery of

the sermon, who began, perhaps, with dis-
cussing some points connected with the common business of the choir, but generally suffered the conversation to stray among still
less appropriate and less excusable topics,
until the occurrence of a jest or witticism
from Charles betrayed them into something
more than a smile, and reduced them to the
necessity of separating from each other, in
order to escape violating the more obvious
decencies of the place.

Then again, it ought not to have been
Charles Williams, of all persons, who scrib-
bled with a lead pencil upon every blank
leaf of every hymn-book and singing-book
within his reach, filling them with grinning
caricatures, with ridiculous mottoes, and
with little messages to the adjoining pew,
some of the occupants of which would blush,
when they found themselves glancing with
greater eagerness at these irregular and un-
seasonable *billets doux*, than listening to more
edifying productions from the pulpit.

And adieu to the composure of that fair
chorister for one morning at least, to whom
Charles Williams presented a bunch of dill,
a pleasant little herb, resembling caraway,
and common in the gardens of New England,
the taste of whose aromatic seeds often
serves in summer to beguile some forlorn
moments that will occur to many attendants
at the meetinghouses of this blessed land, as
well as elsewhere. Not that a gallant attention of this kind from the hands of my
youthful hero occasioned sufficient perturba-
tion in the mind of the receiver to drown her
voice and prevent her from performing her
part in the musical services. On the contrary, such an incident generally had the effect of inspiring her with more than usual
animation, loudness, and expressiveness in
her singing, the cause of which could be con-
jectured by none save such as happened to
unite to an accidental observation a sagacious
philosophy. No other obvious symptoms of
agitation were allowed to escape her watch-
ful self-possession, except perhaps neglect-

ing to keep her snow-white pocket-handkerchief folded up as neatly as usual by the side of her hymn-book, and an inability to recollect the text when she was examined by her decrepit grandmother at home.

Nor were these favours on the part of our leader, in general, very discriminating or partial with respect to their objects. If Charles's bass-viol could have enjoyed a posy of dill, it would often, undoubtedly, have been a successful rival of his more conscious and susceptible mistresses for such attentions. The time had not yet arrived, for the tenderest of all passions to become also, the most overwhelming and absorbing in his soul. He had indeed too much constitutional sensibility not to find on his hands a succession of weekly or monthly idols of his imagination ; but at the same time he had too much juvenile carelessness and too triumphant a presentiment of many exploits yet to be achieved by his genius for music, to allow any very deep and lasting impressions on his heart. Music, praise, and beauty, were to him equally intoxicating subjects of contemplation ; he had not yet had enough of the first two, to admit of his yielding himself entirely up to the influence of the last.

From the few sketches I have already given of the character of this young man, it will not excite surprise in my readers to learn that his parents, his friends, and himself entertained the wish of changing his present sphere and prospects in life. So much notice had been taken of him in various ways ; his general capacity and activity were so conspicuous ; and there was something about him so interesting, apart from his eminence as a young musical performer, that it seemed to be almost a defiance of Providence, to confine him to the obscure profession of a sedentary mechanic.

I use not the word *ignoble,* nor any other term of disparagement or contempt, as applicable to that vocation. I am too sturdy an American for that. Happily, in our country, we have scarcely a conception of what the epithet *ignoble* signifies, except in a purely moral point of view. The aristocratical pride of Europe accounts for this, by insisting, that we are all plebeians together, and of course that distinctions of rank among us are ridiculous. Our own pride, of which we have our full share, accounts for the circumstance on the opposite hypothesis, that we are a nation of highborn noblemen. But this is a poor dispute about names. The truth is, we are neither a nation of noblemen nor plebeians. How can such correlative terms be applied with any shadow of correctness, when the very political relations which they imply, do not exist ? It is using a solecism to call Americans plebeians, because to that class belongs the conscious degradation of witnessing above them, in the same body politic, an order of men born to certain privileges of which they are destitute by birth themselves. And for a similar reason, it is equally a solecism to regard ourselves, even metaphorically, as noblemen.

Why then did Charles Williams and his friends desire him to emerge from the calling in which his youth had been passed ? Oh, we Americans have our *preferences*. We think it an innocent and a convenient thing to draw arbitrary lines of distinction between different professions ; otherwise, the circle of one man's acquaintance would often be oppressively large. It is a pleasant employment, too, to clamber over these distinctions in life. Perhaps there is not a country in the world, where professions are so often changed as in America. We are restless and proud, and since our civil institutions have established no permanent artificial gradations among us, we have devised them ourselves. Yet still it is a matter which we act upon, rather than talk about. No American lady would dare to refuse her neighbour's invitation professedly on the score of the other being beneath her in society. Yet her refusal would be as prompt and decided as any lady's in England, towards an inferior in rank.

I do not wish to analyze too minutely, the aristocratical leaven among us. I do not exactly understand its principle of operation myself. Pedigree it certainly is not, though that perhaps is one of its elements. Wealth and education have something to do with it. Different vocations in life, have much more. Various degress of softness and whiteness of the hands, are perhaps as good criterións as any thing. Certain sets of persons do somehow contrive to obtain an ascendancy in every town and village. But in the present state of society in our country, this whole subject is extremely unsettled. The mass is fermenting, and how the process will result eventually, time only can decide. Probably some future court calendar will rank among the first class of Americar. citizens, all families descended in lines, more or less direct, from former presidents of the nation, heads of departments, governors of states, presidents of colleges, Supreme Court judges, commodores, •and general officers. The second class may

comprehend the posterity of members of
congress, circuit and state judges, clergy-
men, presidents of banks, professors in
colleges, captains of national vessels,
leaders of choirs, and perhaps some others.
I have no curiosity to speculate upon inferi-
or classes, nor to determine any further the
order in which far distant dinners shall be
approached by eaters yet unborn, or future
balls shall be arranged at Washington.

It is a difficult thing to say precisely, how
much my hero was actuated by mere ambition in his wish to change his course of life.
I do not think he despised his paternal employment. *He* had not much reason himself
to complain of the proud man's contumely,
in his own native village. But there were
two strong reasons besides those before
specified, which operated in his father's mind
to determine him on the project of dismissing
his son from his present occupation. One
was, that he was a very unprofitable apprentice. His passion for his favorite art
encroached too largely on his time. A round

of visits and frolics, to which his musical
and companionable qualities exposed him,
absorbed the latter portion of many an afternoon in preparations of dress, and the former part of many a morning in sleeping away
the effects of such expeditions. The other
reason was, that it seemed to be cruel to
confine the lad down to an employment, for
which he had no inclination, and even no
mechanical aptitude. There was little chance
of his ever procuring a generous livelihood
in that employment, and there were other
professions more suited to his excursive and
occasionally bookish disposition. These
would have been sufficient reasons for his
father to make the experiment of some other
course of life for his son, more conformable
to his taste and character, even if paternal
vanity had not whispered into his ear, that
his boy was born for very great things yet !

In New England, before the imposition
of the embargo, and in times of peace, there
were two ways of rising very high in the
world. The one was, to become the clerk

of some wholesale or retail merchant in Boston, and the other, to pass through a college. No aspiring lad throughout the country could think of any other avenue to distinction. Charles Williams was not a lover of money or of trade. He was among the very few youths of his native region, who arrive at the age of thirteen without bartering a pen-knife, or at that of nineteen without cheating or being cheated in the exchange of watches. Accordingly, though he had a distant relative in Boston, who, while yet a minor, had gone four times every year to the market of that metropolis, with a cart full of such assorted commodities as were produced in his native town, and was now one of the wealthiest merchants on the Exchange, Charles obstinately shut his eyes to the prospect of entering this gentleman's counting-house. There was something in literary pursuits much more congenial to the taste and habits of his mind.

With all his follies and eccentricities, he had a warm friend and admirer in the Rev.

Mr Welby, who was for sending *every* young man of the most ordinary capacity to college, that had a soul sufficiently large even barely to meditate on such a purpose. Not that Mr Welby's object, exactly, was to swell the list of liberally educated persons belonging to the place where he was settled, whenever he should communicate to the Massachusetts Historical Society, the topographical and antiquarian account of the town of Waterfield. The propensity in question, rather seemed to be with him a kind of weakness, and one, too, with which many of his profession in New England are afflicted. Owing their own importance in life, and their peculiar opportunities for usefulness to their collegiate education, they have no idea that any greater blessing under the skies can be conferred on an unmarried man of whatever talents, and at whatever age, than causing him to leave the plough or the workshop, and after a struggle of seven years between the Latin dictionary and despair, to obtain a degree. It is not surprising, therefore, that the warm-hearted Mr Welby should offer to become Charles's gratuitous instructer, in preparing him for college ;—an offer which was gratefully accepted.

Although our hero was far from being so apt a scholar in the niceties of the Greek and Latin tongues, as we have already seen him in the science of music, yet the novelty and dignity of the pursuits which he had now adopted, the definite object proposed for him to accomplish, and the shame of abandoning his aim in defeat, unitedly prompted him to undergo one or two years of pretty severe application to study. During this time, he was still a leader of the village choir, though I cannot say that the partial change in his private life and habits, operated in correcting many of those reprehensible characteristics, which I have before lamented as derogatory to our singing-pew.* And al-

* I had some thoughts of describing a few of the effects which Charles's new mode of life, and new topics of consciousness and reputation produced on his

though we had been long taught to anticipate his departure, yet words can scarcely represent the sorrow and dismay with which we bade him farewell on the Sabbath before his setting off for Dartmouth College.

On the next morning at daybreak, a few of us were at his father's threshold to shake hands with him once more. He had already breakfasted, and had mounted the horse which was purchased for the occasion, to be disposed of again on the best terms possible, when he should have entered college. A huge pair of saddlebags, the heir loom of his family for several generations, hung across the horse behind, and contained some changes of wearing apparel, together with his books, and various articles of pastry for the road, which he owed to the care of his sis-

behaviour in private company; but the sketch might clash a little with a picture of a young farmer fitting for college, which now lies by me in an unfinished MS. history of a country academy in New England, and which may possibly hereafter be presented to the public.

ters, and some of their female friends. He
had already repeated his salutations to his
moist-eyed family and acquaintances, and
was holding the reins in his left hand ready
to start, when, at a signal from him, I reach-
ed him his bass-viol, enclosed in a large
leathern case made by his good father, for
the purpose. He received it in his trembling right hand with a look, gleaming through
his agitated countenance, which seemed to
say, I leave not *every* friend behind,—and
spurred off his horse up the margin of the
river.

'And who was the next leader of the
choir ?' is a question, which, (may I humbly
hope ?) these memoirs have excited sufficient interest in my susceptible readers to
propose. With great diffidence I am per-
suaded to answer that it was their humble
servant. Who or what I am, separately
from my once having discharged the honorable function just mentioned, it is of no sort
of consequence to know, and it is clear from
my anonymous title-page, that I do not think

the knowledge would contribute to the eclat
of my humble production. If any lines in
the following portrait of myself appear to be
favorably drawn, let not vanity be ascribed
to the act, while I seek to hide the original,
and even his very name, from the public
gaze.

Previously to the departure of my friend
Charles Williams, I had acted as player of
clarionet to the choir ; not, I fear, always
with the greatest reputation ; for I scarcely
remember a Sunday of my performance,
when my instrument did not at least once
through the day betray itself into a hideous
squeak as involuntary on my part as if there
had been a little evil spirit within the tube,
sent there to tempt and torment me. At
these agonizing moments, I would cast one
glance at the countenance of Charles Williams, and finding that there was in that
image of native civility no mark of fretful
reprehension, or of tittering infirmity, I
proceeded in my part ;—nor do I know how
I discovered that my fellow singers were not

quite so composed as their leader, unless it
were, that while from alarm and mortification, my face was reddening, and my perspiration flowing, my eyes were enlarged from
the same cause, and thus extended the sphere
of their lateral vision.   But I am no optician,
and hazard nothing on this point beyond con-
jecture.   I believe it was instinct that prevented me, on such occasions, from seeing
so far as into the adjoining pew.   There
was one face there, on which, if I had- ever
seen a smile approaching to derision, I know
that it would have broken my heart.

But if I do not deceive myself, the squeak
in my clarionet was the only ridiculous
thing about me, and was probably but the
more amusing from its striking contrast to
the general gravity of my deportment.   On
laying aside, therefore, this instrument of
my little disgraces, which was a necessary
step towards my leading the choir with effect
and energy, I trust I had no enormous dis-
qualifications for the office.   The authority
of Charles had been sustained solely by his

transcendant musical talents ; mine, I felt, was to be preserved by the most exemplary demeanour, and an assiduous attention to my duty.   I could only boast of a mediocrity in musical knowledge and vocal execution. If I was far below my predecessor in accomplishments requisite for the office, I at least avoided the mistakes into which Mr Harrington had been often plunged.   Until a calamitous concurrence of circumstances, soon ·to be rehearsed, not an individual, I think, left the choir during my administration, with the exception of those, whom death or removal out of town subtracted from our number.   I loved the office, for it gave me a little importance, and I was, at that time, of no great account in the parish in other respects.   Besides, I was extremely attached to public worship, and to all its hallowed decencies, thinking it an honour to exercise the superintendence over so important a department as that assigned to me.   With regard to punctuality at meeting, (for so we call *church* in New England,) the minister

himself never outstripped me in that particular. He has more than once, on a stormy
day, without commencing service, dismissed
my single self, together with one other pa-
rishioner ,who appeared at meeting only in
such weather, and came then, as he whimsi-
cally alleged, *to fill up ;* and often, on some
of our terribly cold Sundays, when seven or
eight worshippers in leggins would well nigh
drown the preacher's voice with the prodigious knocking and stamping of their feet, I
was found alone at my post in the singing-
gallery, suffering in perfect silence the ago-
ny of my frost-bitten extremities, and permit-
ing my attention to be no further diverted
from Mr Welby, thannow and then in watch-
ing the dense volumes of congealed vapour,
that were breathed out from a few scattered
pews in the almost vacant edifice.

So far as I can impartially judge, I was
one of the most peaceable and unpretending
of men. I gave out always, without the
least hesitation, whatever tune was suggested to me by any individual in the choir,

sacrificing with pleasure my own little preferences, and what is more, the pride of
authority, to the gratification of others.
Perhaps the general manners of the choir
at church were improved during my precentorship. Let me with modesty say, and
with deference to the shade of my dear
friend Charles, who is now no more, that
my own example probably contributed to
some slight amendment in our body after his
departure. I had long since formed a secret
resolution in my breast, that no old man in
the congregàtion should be more attentive to
the services than myself, and I carried it
into effect. This naturally influenced a few
of my immediate companions to adopt a
similar deportment ; and the good order of
the rest of the choir suffered at least only a
negative violation from the sleep of some,
and the studies of others, who preferred look-
ing over the tunes of the Village Harmony,
or reading the everlasting elegy on Sophro-
nia, or amusing themselves with the inscrip-
tions of their late leader, to receiving the

benefits which might have been derived from Mr Welby's excellent sermons.

After a year had glided away very nearly in this manner, some sensation was produced in the choir and congregation, and, ultimately, some disturbance occasioned to my own peace and happiness, by the addition of a gentleman to our number, who, on several accounts, had no small pretensions. He was the preceptor of an academy, situated, if I recollect aright, not more than ten miles from the town of Waterfield. He was paying his addresses to a young lady of this last mentioned place, and therefore seized on the opportunities which a remission of his duties every Saturday afternoon allowed him, to visit the object of his affections. The Sabbath, of course, was spent by him in our village, and as he was a professed admirer and performer of sacred music, and was a gentleman of liberal education, genteel though forward manners, and a superior style of dress for a country town, he was soon introduced into the singing-pew, and

without the least difficulty found a seat at my
left hand. Being blest with a happy degree
of modest assurance, it did not require a
second invitation for him to assume habitual-
ly the same place afterwards as a matter of
course.

On the very first Sabbath that he joined
us, he startled me a little by requesting that
Old Hundred might be sung to a psalm which
the minister had just begun to read. I told
him that I should be very glad to oblige him
by announcing that tune to the choir, but the
truth was, it had not been performed in our
meetinghouse probably for thirty years ; —
that there were but four or five singers who
were acquainted with it, being such only as
had chanced to hear it sung at home by their
fathers or grandfathers, and that those few
had only practised it once or twice together
and in private, from mere curiosity to ascertain how so celebrated a piece of musical
antiquity would sound.

'Oh, if there are four or five,' replied
Mr Forehead, (the name of my lofty new

acquaintance) 'who know any thing of Old Hundred, by all means let us have it. I beg it, Sir, as a particular favour, and will give you my reasons for the request after service.'

My prevailing disposition to oblige, and the great quantity of time already consumed in our conversation, imposed upon me now the necessity of pronouncing aloud, as was usual just before beginning to sing, the name of this venerable air. No sooner had the word proceeded from my mouth, than there appeared to be a motion of keen curiosity among the congregation below, but in the choir around me there reigned the stillness of incredulity and surprise. All the elder members of the flock, I could observe, looked upwards to the gallery, with the gleams of pleasurable expectation in their countenances. Of our well-filled orchestra, only eight individuals arose, for there were no more among us, who possessed the least acquaintance with Old Hundred. And even three out of that number were as ignorant of it as those who continued seated, but ventured to expose themselves, trusting to the assistance they might derive from the voices of the other performers, and from the score of the tune itself, contained in some, though I think not in all of the copies of the Village Harmony which were present.

The psalm was sung with tolerable correctness; but accompanied with *such* a fanning on the part of the females, who were all sitting, and *such* a whispering among those of the correlative sex who were unemployed, that I could bode nothing but disturbance and unhappiness for a long time to come in our choral circle.

During the reading of the next psalm, while Mr Forehead was alarming me with a recommendation to sing St Martin's, four stout acquaintances of my own pressed forward and whispered with an earnestness that carried the sound over every part of the edifice, 'Sing New Jerusalem!' New Jerusalem therefore I appointed to be sung, and thus prevented, as I make no sort of question, more than three quarters of the singers from leaving their seats vacant in the afternoon.

At the close of the morning service, I had the promised interview and explanation with my new acquaintance. It seems that since leaving college he had been reading law for a year in an office at one of our seaport towns, and while there, had occasionally assisted in the choir of some congregation, into which had been introduced a new and purer taste for sacred music than generally prevailed through the rest of the country. In that choir, as he informed me, no tunes of American origin were ever permitted to gain entrance. Fugues there were a loathing and detestation. None but the slow, grand, and simple airs which our forefathers sang, found any indulgence. Mr Forehead assured me that no other music was worth hearing, and what seemed to weigh particularly with him was the circumstance, that the slow music in question was beginning to be in the fashion. It was under the operation of these ideas that he had been so strenuous in forcing upon our choir the performance of Old Hundred and St Martin's, in defiance of our helpless ignorance of both of them.

It appeared to me that his zeal on this point was carrying him too far. I saw in his aims quite as strong workings of a conscious superiority in taste and of the fastidious arrogance of fashion, as a love for genuine and appropriate music. I could not but question, too, the propriety of suddenly and violently forcing upon a choir and congregation a species of music to which they were entirely unaccustomed. It occurred to me, besides, that though the most slow and solemn tunes might be executed with good effect when sustained by the accompaniment of an organ, yet it was scarcely judicious to confine the whole music of a *vocal* choir entirely or even principally to that kind alone. But all these suggestions were of no avail in convincing my opponent, and we parted with not the kindest opinions and feelings respecting each other.

In the course of a month, Mr Forehead's arguments, persuasion, and example, wrought in a large portion of the choir a very considerable change of taste on this subject. There were some, who loved novelty ; there were others, who yielded to the stranger's assurances respecting the fashionableness of the thing ; and there was a third description, who were really convinced of the better adaptation of the ancient tunes to the purposes of worship, and had a taste to enjoy their solemn and beautiful strains. All these classes composed perhaps about a moiety of the choir, and were eager for the introduction of the good old music. The other half were extremely obstinate and almost bigoted in their opposition to this measure, and in their attachment to the existing catalogue of tunes. Disputes now ran high amongst us. Most of us took sides on the question with an inexcusable warmth, and without any attempt at compromise.

I know of nothing more unconquerable and spiteful than the bickerings of a divided

choir while they last. In addition to all the
ordinary exacerbations of party spirit, there
is a most unpardonable offence committed
by each side in suspecting the good taste of
the other. Thus vanity is wounded to its
deepest core, and conscience and conviction
are fretted into a fierce perseverance, which
is not at all diminished by the circumstance,
that the parties must sit, act, and sing in
the closest contact, and almost breathe into
each other's faces.

In the midst of this unhappy musical com-
motion, there was one individual, who had
the good fortune to remain thus far entirely
neuter. It was, reader, the humble historian
of these transactions,—the afflicted leader of
that agitated band. I had long wished, together with my friend Charles Williams,
that a better style of music might prevail
amongst us. But we felt that we had neither skill nor authority to effect the exchange.
If the tares should be torn up, we knew
that the wheat would be liable to come with
them. My private opinion, as well as

general disposition, led me therefore, to be as quiescent as possible amid the difficulties now existing. I did not, as I believe, escape all censure from either party, but I received no bitter treatment from any one. Due deference and acknowledgment still continued for some time to be paid me as leader, except perhaps from the pragmatical stranger. But no efforts or prudence on my part could prevent the explosion which was ultimately to ensue.

When it was found that Mr Forehead had sufficient influence to introduce a few of his favourite tunes on the settled and customary catalogue, and that the matter had proceeded to something more than a simple experiment, the admirers of fugues looked upon themselves as a beaten party, and took occasion, when two of the obnoxious airs had happened to be given out by me on one Sunday morning, to absent themselves altogether from worship in the afternoon. My feelings in this predicament are not to be described. I regarded myself as a principal cause of this deplorable feud, and lamented. that I had not had sufficient strength of mind to resist the encroachments of the active gentleman at my left hand. But the standard was now raised and war was declared. I felt that it would be ignominious to quit my post. I gave up for a time my arguments with Mr Forehead on the propriety of singing slow tunes altogether. No attempts were made to effect a reconciliation and return of the absenting party. It was resolved among those who remained behind, to perform no other music than such as we deemed the most genuine, and an express was sent off by the first opportunity to purchase thirty copies of the lately published * * * * * * * Collection.

In the mean time, however, the controversy had descended to the congregation. As long as the choir had kept together on terms of seeming decency, it was hardly to be expected that the audience at large would take part in our little animosities. The parish would never have undertaken to con-

trol a whole choir, if that choir would have
united in any species of music, however
contrary to the tastes and habits of those
who bore no share in its performance. But
when it was found that our little vocal com-
monwealth had been rent asunder, and that
so large a division of malcontents had retired
in indignation to a Sacred Mount, the sympathies of brothers, sisters, parents, and
friends, were at once excited, and musical
predilections were enlisted along with the
ties of nature to swell the threatening
dissatisfaction. For several Sundays I remained firm, supported as I was by all the
ostentatious influence and patronage of Mr
Forehead, and the zealous cooperation of
his partizans. We persisted every Sabbath
in singing these five tunes—Old Hundred,
St Martin's, Mear, Bath, and Little Mal-
borough, unless the minister varied his me-
tres from that standard, and even then we
were prepared with tunes of a similar class.
By these means we hoped to awaken a better taste among those of the congregation

who were averse to our new style, and
eventually to recall a majority of the dissi-
dents, who we trusted would become convinced of the excellence of our improvements, and gradually return to partake of
the honour and pleasure attached to them.

But our expectations were disappointed.
Our triumph had a date of only about three
months, and was even waning while it last-
ed. We could not force the likings of a
prejudiced, and in some respects, exasperat-
ed congregation. The singing in the meetinghouse was the constant topic of every
private conversation. All possible ridicule
and contempt were thrown out against each
of the respective styles in question. All
sorts of arguments were used, that reason,
or passion, or prejudice, could devise. Till
at length, I verily believe, our inclinations
became so perverted by the mere operation
of party feeling, that many of us hated and
despised the venerable air of Old Hundred
with as much heartiness as they did the toad
that crossed their path at twilight, while

others regarded the generally very innocent tune of Northfield with the same abhorrence that we bestowed on a snake. Unfortunately for the better side of the argument at this time, the attachment to a rapid, fuguing, animated style of singing was too deeply and extensively seated in the affections of the people of Waterfield, to be eradicated by the impotent perseverance of our diminished choir. Pew after pew became deserted, until we found that we were singing, and Mr Welby preaching almost to naked walls. The hoary head was still there, for it loved to listen to the strains which had nourished the piety of its youth. A few families of fashionable pretensions encouraged us, for there was something aristocratical in the superior taste of our newly introduced music, and something modish in its reputation. Nothing but the strongest religious feelings induced a few other scattered individuals to appear at meeting, and it was but too evident that full three quarters of the usual attendants remained at home.

This spectacle produced the deepest effect on my mind. I had a sufficient sense of the blessings of public worship to feel and know, that they must not be sacrificed to a mere point of musical taste. I was therefore perfectly willing to resign all my biases for the sake of seeing our beloved meetinghouse again filled with its motley throngs, and of feeling the delicious, though perhaps imaginary coolness excited by the agitations of several hundred fans, those busy little agents, so lively, so glancing, yet so silent,—and of hearing the full thunder of all the seats as they were slammed down after prayer, though Mr Welby had frequently remonstrated with earnestness against it,—but much to my satisfaction, remonstrated in vain, for I scarcely know many sounds more grateful to my ear than this. Whether it is, that it is connected with the idea of a full congregation, which I always loved, or with the close of the prayer, which in early youth I thought insufferably long, or whether it was originally a most agreeable diversification of

the inaction and monotony of church hours,
I cannot tell, but something has wonderfully
attached me to the noise of a thousand falling seats. And this attachment you will
find very general in New England. Many
a minister there will tell you that his attempts
to correct the supposed evil have always
been ineffectual ; and if you are riding
through the land on a summer Sabbath, you
may observe that long before you are in
sight of a meetinghouse, your starting horse
and saluted ear will give decided testimony
to the clergyman's complaint, while all the
wakened echoes round will inform you that
if you spur forward for a half mile or more,
you will be in season to hear a good portion
of the sermon, though you have lost the
prayer.

I was unable any longer to endure the
destitute appearance of the meetinghouse,
and having consulted with Mr Welby, who
advised me to make whatever sacrifices I
could for the restoration of peace, I caused
it to be circulated one day in the village,

that on the following Sabbath I should return to the kind of music which had lately been abandoned. The necessity for this measure was the more pressing, as I heard it murmured that a town-meeting was soon to be called for the purpose of securing a mode of singing, which should be agreeable to a great majority of the parish.

My present associates and supporters, indeed, almost to a man, took umbrage at my determination ; and were not seen in public when the Sabbath came. But I was surrounded by all the choristers of the other party, and the meetinghouse was crowded, and the downfalling seats rebellowed again to my delighted ear.

And now for several weeks was the full-breathing triumph of the lovers of crotchets and quavers over the votaries of minims and semibreves. The latter faction sullenly absented themselves from the singing pew, and generally from worship, while the former revelled amid the labyrinths of fugues, believing to their own happiness, certainly, the

order of consecutive parts to be the sweetest
of melodies, and the recurrence of consecutive fifths the most delightful of harmonies.
In place of the lists of ancient tunes above
enumerated, were now substituted Russia,
Northfield, The Forty Sixth Psalm, New
Jerusalem, and others of the same mint.
The name of Billings was a sufficient pass-
port of recommendation to any air that was
mentioned, while that of Williams or of
Tansur, was sure to condemn it to neglect.
We were encouraged by the looks and
voices of all those members of the congregation who were beneath fifty years of age,
or if any such declined to accompany us
either with a hum or an articulated modula-
tion, they perhaps testified their satisfaction
by the visible beating of a hand, whose arm
lay along the top of a pew.

But this was to me only a silver age,
compared with the golden reign of Charles
Williams. I felt that my taste had become
much confirmed and purified by my recent
study and practice of a better style of church

music, and I could therefore the less easily
tolerate that which I was compelled now to
support. By far the better half of the choir,
also, in point of musical skill and execution,
refrained from renewing their services, and I
was distressed to know what methods I
could adopt to allure them back. Even my
rival and annoyer, Mr Forehead, I should
have been glad to welcome again at my left
hand. His voice had both power and
sweetness, and perhaps the only defect in
his mode of performing, was his perpetual
attempt at ornament and trilling, a defect,
still further enhanced by the circumstance,
that instead of trilling with his tongue, he
always attempted that accomplishment with
his lips alone, being the veritable original,
by whom the well known unhappy change
was made upon the word *bow* in the following
distich.

> ' With reverence let the saints appear,
>   And bow before the Lord.'

Nevertheless, I was perfectly willing and
desirous to enter into a negotiation with

him and his party, for the purpose of procuring, if possible, some mutual compromise and reconciliation, and filling up again the complement of the choir.

But this was an attempt of no little delicacy and difficulty. The exasperation of both parties was too recent and too sore, immediately to admit of an amicable personal union, or to allow the expectation that either side would endure the favorite music of the other. Time, however, which effects such mighty revolutions in the affairs of empires, condescends also to work the most important changes in the aspect of humble villages, and still humbler choirs.

It is the office of this unpretending narrative to record the mutations to which one of the last mentioned communities is exposed in New England. Whether the train of incidents here exhibited be a specimen of what occurs to many other choirs within the same region, my experience does not enable me to decide. Many of my readers, however, will probably recognise in these memoirs of a single collection of singers, several features common to all others.

I have often thought that such communities are a kind of arena for the exhibition of some peculiar and specific human infirmities. Every new combination of our social nature, indeed, seems to produce some new results, in the same manner as each species of vegetables nourishes its peculiar tribe of animalcules. I take it that our National Congress elicits from its component members certain specific virtues and vices, and certain modifications of feeling, passion, and talent, denied to us mere readers of newspapers at home. Where but on the floor of the American Capitol, would the peculiarities of a certain member's sarcasm, and of another member's sublime statesmanship be generated and developed ? So in a church choir, there somehow arise certain shades of freaks, certain starts of passion, certain species of whim, certain modes of folly, and let me humbly suggest, also, certain descriptions of virtue, to be found exactly in no other specimens throughout the moral kingdom of man.

May I fondly hope, that these desultory delineations, intermingled though they are with intrusive speculations, and superficial efforts at philosophizing, may at least prove corrective of kindred defects, if such any where exist, with those which are here exposed ? A mirror sometimes shocks the child out of a passion of whose deformity he could not be convinced except by its disgusting effects on his own face. And if the perusal of these pages, which have been too carelessly thrown together, in order to indulge some juvenile recollections, and to sooth some painful, heavy hours, be instrumental in correcting any imperfections to which our church-choirs are liable, I shall feel more than repaid for my anxiety in undertaking the perilous enterprise of authorship. But let us be moving forward.

In a very few months, negotiations were entered into, with the body of the other party, of whom some half dozen individuals of the least zealous had from time to time returned, and given in their adhesion to the ruling powers, The truth was, that on our part, we felt extremely the want of instrumental music, and a few excellent voices on the treble. After Charles Williams had left us, a tolerable bass-viol was played by an elderly storekeeper, a bachelor, who had formerly assisted the choir several years with that instrument, but had resigned it as soon as Charles became prepared to supply his place. This gentleman, with his clerk, who played a fine flute, had participated in the dudgeon of the lovers of ancient melody. But nearly all of them now wished to return, conscious, undoubtedly, of the improvement which it was truly in their power to contribute to our performances, and unwilling that their talents should any longer be hidden in a napkin.

The terms of reconciliation and reunion were settled in the following manner. As our performances were required regularly five times on a Sabbath, it was agreed that the arrangement of tunes throughout the day should be two fugues, two of the slow

ancient airs, and one of a different description from either.   Neither party could well
object to airs of a rapid and animated movement, in which all the parts continued unin-
terruptedly to the close, as in the case with
Wells, Windham, Virginia, and many others.   Another class of tunes, also, were
very general favourites, though they avoided
both extremes that were the bones of con-
tention among us.   I allude to those, in
which the third line is a duett between the
bass and treble, of which St Sebastian's is a
well-known beautiful instance.

For some time, we proceeded together in
this new arrangement with as little interruption as could be well expected from existing
circumstances.   A very few of the most
obstinate and paltry minded, of each side,
held out indeed for longer or shorter periods,
and one or two perhaps never returned till a
grand revolution of the whole corps to be
described hereafter, should our history ever
reach a second part.   For several Sundays,
also, four or five Guelphs would contemptu-

ously sit in perfect silence during the singing
of the Ghibeline tunes, and as many Ghibe-
lines would return the compliment during
the singing of the Guelph tunes.   And even
when they were compelled to abandon such
indecent deportment by the censures to
which it exposed them, to my certain knowledge they were silent while standing up with
the choir, or moved their lips in a whisper,
or sang so very low, as to give no sort of
assistance to the rest.

However, these little factious symptoms
gradually disappeared, and I had at length
the happiness of finding myself at the head
of my musical flock, with the embers of
former grievances well nigh asleep, and with
a decided advantage gained in our taste and
selection of tunes.   But what struggles and
dangers had been incurred in order to arrive
at this improved condition !   I can resort to
no illustration of these events more apt than
the kingdom of France, which, as some imagine, derives a faint compensation for the hor-
rors of the revolution, from the amendments

effected in some of its circumstances and institutions, that neither despotism, nor superstition, can in future hope to wipe away.

Yet, amid these various concussions, it will not be surprising that my own authority should have been completely undermined. It is scarce supposable that I could be a very decided favourite with either of the parties who had frowned so awfully upon each other, since I had in a manner sided with both of them. Although, therefore, I was most scrupulously impartial in selecting such descriptions of tunes as exactly conformed to the terms of the treaty, yet there was not a member of the choir, whose friendship was sufficiently zealous to join me in resisting the new encroachments of Mr Forehead. While that gentleman confined himself to a general selection equally impartial with mine, not a spectator thought of murmuring, when he suggested, as he constantly did, this and that particular tune for any given psalm or hymn ; and suggested it, too, with such an air of certainty and confidence, that I was not the man to hold up my head, and say at a single glance, ' Sir, I am on my own ground here.' When he found that his suggestions were in this way constantly adopted, it was an easy and natural transition for him next to whisper round of his own accord, to the few who sat near him, the name of the tune to be sung, and to whisper it also to me with the same non-chalance, that I might proclaim it to the choir as usual. And then, with as much ease and as calm a face as Napoleon wore when he stept from the consular chair to the imperial throne, it only remained for him to assume the precentorship at once, by uttering aloud, one Sunday, to my amazement, the name of the first tune in the morning, and continuing the practice from that moment until his departure from the choir and the neighbourhood.

Thus, my own occupation was gone. On the afternoon of the morning just mentioned, I entered the singing pew, and took my seat at some distance from the post of honour, which I felt was no longer mine. It was of no use to appeal to the members of the choir in my defence. I had suffered encroachment after encroachment to be gradually made upon my authority, until the last act of usurpation was scarcely perceptible. I knew that I could have no enthusiastic supporters of my rights. I had not one personal qualification by which to balance the imposing and overbearing accomplishments of my competitor. I dare say all the choir and all the congregation thought him the best leader, as I confess, on the whole, he was. Probably the precise circumstances under which the exchange was made, were not discerned by many among them. Perhaps they might have supposed, that my resignation and transfer of the pitchpipe were voluntary. Indeed I half hope they did suppose so. But no—I am willing they should have known the whole truth. But let the matter rest. It is an era in my biography which I do not love to contemplate.

I am not ashamed, however, that I continued in the choir. I am certain it was not meanness which kept me there, though some at first sight may so interpret it. It was a struggle between pride and duty, in which duty won the victory—and though pride had indignation for its ally, yet my devoted and disinterested love for those singing seats, came up to the assistance of duty, and decided the contest.

Besides, why should I desert those seats ? Should I have felt happier,—could I have concealed my mortification better, by sitting with the family below ? By no means. I might as well remain where I was, and bury my feelings in the flood of sound with which my own tremulous voice was mingled.

For I considered, that it was always my peculiar lot, wherever I was, and whatever I did, to have some mortification or other on my hands, or, I would say, on my heart. The squeak of my clarionet was but an epitome of a certain note that has occasionally grated the whole tenor of my fortune and life. I had a disaffected mother-in-law. My school master was partial to my rival. I was bound an apprentice to an uncongenial employment, which I could not abandon until I was free. I was once jilted. How I was superseded in the choir, has been seen above. I always try to do my best, but am liable to overdo. I have been disinterested and generous to my friends, till I have spoiled them, and they have sometimes become my foes from expecting more than I could or ought to perform. The same out-of-the-way note, I acknowledge, attaches itself to most of my compositions. I have written some things in these very pages of a kin with that portentous strain of my instrument ; but I could not help it ; and I expect, that with some praises that may be vouchsafed to this production, other things will be said of it that will cut me to the very heart. But I will try to be prepared for them.

And now, reader, you may in some measure understand how I could endure to haunt, like a ghost, the scene of my former triumphs. Remember, however, that I met no scorn on the occasion. Not a soul was there, who would not have regretted my absence. A gentle and quiet exchange of leaders had been effected, and there the matter rested in every mind. The most direct way by which I could have caused it to redound to my ill-reputation and discomfort, would have been, to make a stir about it. Prudence, therefore, if nothing else, might whisper me the proper course to be pursued.

Thus a fifth leader of the choir at Water-field is duly and regularly recorded on these veracious annals. His reign, like that of his predecessor, was stormy and unfortunate. For some weeks, Mr Forehead adhered inviolably to the articles of union touching the selection of particular kinds of music. But it is the natural tendency of usurped power, when thus easily acquired, to produce security, audacity, encroachment, downfal. The precentor's partialities at length began to burst out, and occasional small violations of the treaty were hazarded with impunity. But when he attempted to advance further, and one whole Sunday passed without the assignment of a single fugue to wake up the indifferent congregation, an alarm was taken by the lovers of that species of melody. A repetition of former disturbances and irritations was threatened. Some of the choir took no part in the performance ; some absolutely left the seats for neighbouring pews, and a convulsion was on the eve of again breaking us in pieces.

The amiable Mr Welby perceived the indications of an approaching storm. He devoted himself, therefore, the ensuing week, to the preparation of a discourse, which he hoped might check the evil in its commencement. Meanwhile, however, the difficulty was provided for in another way. A deputation had called on the existing leader that very evening, and, making the strongest representations of the dissatisfaction which would certainly prevail, if he should continue the course of administration to which he was inclined, extorted from him a promise that he would immediately return to the recent arrangement which had so well secured the harmony of the choir, and the complacency of the congregation.

But Mr Welby knew nothing of the happy turn that affairs had thus assumed, and the members of the choir, on their part, knew nothing of the benevolent officiousness that was prompting the labours of his study. Even had he been aware that a reconciliation had taken place, it is probable that he would still have interwoven into his next discourse some gentle persuasives to mutual kindness. His utter ignorance, however, of that happy occurrence, caused his sermon in some places to wear an aspect of unnecessary pointedness and severity. Although it contained but one explicit allusion to the choir, yet it unfortunately was calculated with exquisite skill to meet precisely such a state of excitement as there was every reason to suppose the singers would by this time be wrought up to. But what was meant for exhortation, was now felt as reproach ; the more tender and soothing the preacher's language, the more it seemed like oil de-

scending on the flames. The whole choir
had come together that morning in a state of
jealous irritability ; they were ready to
break out somewhere ; the terms of the last
Sunday evening's engagement guarded them
from waging battle with each other ; the one
party were moody and disappointed, the
other felt injured and suspicious ; 'and now,
to be held up to the congregation—to be
found fault with by the minister—to be chid-
den just at the moment when they were all
endeavouring to keep peace together ! '—
Such were the exaggerated and unjust reflections excited in their minds by one of the
mildest and most beautiful discourses on
brotherly love, that were ever composed, and
in which, as I before observed, only one
direct allusion was made to them, wherein
the preacher expressed his trust, that those
who gladdened the house of God with the
harmony of their voices, would be particularly careful to cultivate the much sweeter,
and to the ear of Heaven, the much more
acceptable harmony, that resulted from a
union of pious hearts.

But no matter, it gave to those prejudiced and capricious choristers an object on which to exercise their characteristic waywardness, and an opportunity to make themselves of some troublesome importance. Accordingly, to wreak a glorious revenge on the interfering parson, and to impress on the whole world a sense of their immeasurable consequence, not a soul of them on the afternoon of that day appeared in the singing seats—with the exception, let me humbly add, of *one*, as unworthy indeed as the rest, but who would never for such a provocation, have deserted that gallery until the imitation-marble columns that supported it were crumbling into ruins. Whatever others might have thought of me, however poor-spirited and grandmother-loving I may have appeared, yet if there have been any moments in my life of loftier triumph, but at the same time, of more piteous melancholy than others, they assuredly occurred during the quarter of an hour, when I sat perfectly alone in that deserted singing-pew, fixing my eye

and face on no other object than my afflicted
minister, who was waiting in trembling dismay for the entrance of the rest of the choir.

Never shall I forget the moment when the
dreadful truth flashed into his mind, and he
perceived, by their protracted absence, the
mistake that he must have committed in the
morning. Yet it was but an instant of ago-
ny, and was succeeded by a high-souled
though involuntary look of calmness, and
consciousness that he had discharged no
more than a well-meant religious and professional duty. The tears were soon wiped
away from his face, a decent composure was
assumed, a hymn was quickly selected,
which Watts, the sweet psalmist of the mod-
ern Israel, could furnish him most appropri-
ately for the occasion, and was then announced and read with a tremulousness of voice,
that indicated rather a successful effort for
firmness, than any yielding weakness of
heart.

I had the honor, on that occasion, of setting and leading a tune, which was accom-

panied by Mr Welby's modest, though perfect and full-toned bass. We were the only
singers for the remainder of that day. The
hearts of some among the worshippers were
too full, and of others too anxious, to lend
us a helping note. From that moment, the
closest friendship was formed and cemented
between Mr Welby and myself, and it was
but lately that I paid him the last dollar of
the money which he liberally advanced to
defray more than half the expenses of my
college education.

I was 'monarch of all I survey'd' in that
singing-pew for four months. Mr Welby
of course had no apology to make. Apology
indeed ! He was in truth the only injured
party. Had the whole choir entered the
meetinghouse on their knees, singing *Pecca-
vimus* and *Miserere*, they would, by such hu-
miliation, have scarcely effaced their violation
of sacred proprieties and of the feelings of
their pastor. Should Mr Welby's Journal of
his Ministry, which I know he has copiously
recorded, be ever given to the world, I have

not a doubt that this transaction will be stated there with ample justice and candour, and make no insignificant appearance among the various trials which a New England Clergyman is called to endure.

It was long ere a sense of lingering compunction, together with various other feelings and circumstances, brought the wanderers back to their deserted fold. Meanwhile I continued the discharge of my solitary duty in the gallery, and was most minutely scrupulous in selecting the tunes according to the arrangement prescribed amidst the recent troubles. I was determined to give to no person whatever the slightest cause of offence, but to hold out every encouragement for all who chose to return. Mr Welby and myself derived occasional assistance from a few voices below, but often the whole musical duties of worship devolved upon us alone. Few indeed of the members of the late choir carried their animosity so far as to renounce attendance at church altogether. Mr Forehead, I think, was never seen in that meet-

inghouse but once again. Soon after his
abrupt retirement from the seats, he married
and left the neighbourhood, carrying off with
him one of the best treble voices in the village.

At the beginning of the following winter, I
was compelled to fulfil an engagement that
I had incurred, to keep a district-school for
three months in the county of Rockingham,
New Hampshire. Soon after I had taken
my departure for this purpose, Mr Welby
was seized with a troublesome affection of
his lungs, which scarcely permitted him to
perform even his strictly pastoral services.
And now the musical tide in my native congregation was at its very lowest ebb. For
two or three Sundays the minister did not
even presume to read a psalm, certain that
no one present would rise and sing it. Can
my readers imagine from what quarter relief
was derived in this gloomy state of things?
From none other than a few of the very
oldest members of the congregation. Four
ancient men, the least of whose ages was
seventy-three, indignant at the folly and per-

tinacity of those singers of yesterday, and
wearied out with waiting for a return of
tolerable music, tottered up the stairs one
Sabbath morning with the assistance of the
panelled railing, and took their places in
the seats left vacant by their degenerate
grandsons.   Two of them had fought in the
old French war, and all had taken a civil or
military part, more or less conspicuous, in
the struggle for our country's independence.
One indeed, bore a title of considerable
military rank.   His hair was as white as
the falling snow ; the other three displayed
white or grey wigs, with a large circular
bush, mantling over the upper part of the
back, like a swelling cloud round the shoulders of old Wachusett.   Their voices of
course were broken and tremulous, but not
destitute of a certain grave and venerable
sweetness.   They kept the most perfect
time, as they stood in a row, fronting the
minister, with their hands each holding a
lower corner of their books, which they
waved from side to side in a manner the

most solemn and imposing. Their very
pronunciation had in it something primitive
and awe-inspiring. Their *shall* broadened
into *shawl*, *do* was exchanged for *doe*, and
earth for *airth*. Their selection of tunes
was of the most ancient composition and
slowest movement, with the exception, occasionally, of old Sherburne, and the Thirty
Fourth Psalm.

How vividly do I remember the spectacle
which they presented to my revering eyes,
when I attended the meetinghouse late one
morning, after having walked on snow-shoes
the last five miles of the distance from the
place where I was employed in teaching, to
pay a short visit to my friends. On entering
the beloved edifice, whose white, though
bell-less steeple I had for some time gazed on
from afar with emotions almost as strong as
if I had been absent several years, it was
my purpose to ascend immediately to my
usual station. But before I had passed the
door, unexpected and unaccustomed sounds
for that place burst upon my ears, and my

curiosity irresistibly led me forward to my father's pew near the pulpit, that I might have a full view of the strange choir which had so magically sprung up during my short absence, and that I might not disturb it by my unnecessary intrusion.

This was not the first nor the last time that I have witnessed extraordinary energy of character, as occasions called for it, displayed by octogenarians of New England. Few of my readers, perhaps, will fail to remember instances analogous to that here recorded. Those apparently decrepit forms, which you see at frame-raisings, confined to the easy task of fashioning the pins, and telling stories of the revolution, or about the door in winter, mending the sled and gathering sticks for the fire ; or drawing the rake in summer after the moving hay-cart, occasionally surprise you by the exhibition of an activity and strength, which you would think they must have forever resigned. Who can tell how much this latent vigour of theirs may be owing to our bracing climate, joined to the effects of their former stirring life, and particularly to the influence of those preternatural exertions, which they, with the whole country, once put forth in the war of independence ? I thought I distinctly saw, in the efforts of those seniors of my native parish to supply it with sacred music, something of that spirit which had sprung to arms, when the necessities of their country and the voice of Heaven bade them forego every personal convenience, and take up their march to Charlestown, to Cambridge, and to the heights of Dorchester. Ye laurelled old men ! ye saviours of your country, and authors of unimaginable blessings for your posterity ! ye shall not descend to your graves, without the fervent thanks, the feeble tribute of one, who often in his thought refers his political enjoyments and hopes to your principle, your valour, and your blood.

How soon will it be ere a revolutionary veteran will be seen no more among us ! It is with a feeling of melancholy and desolation that I perceive their number irrevocably lessening every year. We do not half enough load the survivors with grateful honours. * We ought formally and publicly to cherish them with more pious assiduity. Their pensions are an insufficient recompense of their merits, for the plain reason that they scarcely fought for mercenary considerations. Even those who expected pay, and sometimes could not obtain it from the continental treasury, would have died rather than touch the gold of the enemy. On the anniversaries of our independence, I would therefore assign to all who had any share in accomplishing the revolution, a distinct place in our civic processions. The orator of the day should add interest to his performance by an address to their venerable corps. They should be escorted to the festive hall, they should be entertained as honoured guests, they should be toasted,

* This paragraph, as well as the whole book, was written a year before the Bunker Hill Monument Celebration.

and the toast should be drunk standing, and the chaplain of the day should offer prayers for their long and uninterrupted happiness, both in this world and the next.

But this last idea brings me round again to the reverend choir, on which was fastened the other end of my chain of patriotic reflections. Those of my readers, who are interested as much in the links of a dynasty as in the more general facts of a history, may wish to know who was regarded as the leader among that group of antiques. And the question is pertinent enough. For although they were too far advanced in years beyond the miserable vanities of musical pretension, and were now too much on a mutual level in point of abilities or skill, to be actuated by any aspiring ambition, yet they had also too much experience in the affairs of life, not to be aware of the necessity of some ostensible head, in order to manage even the humblest common concern with requisite harmony and effect. The person, therefore, whom, rather by a tacit, reciprocal understanding, than any formal nomination, or elective acclamation, they made choice of for their conductor, was Colonel John Wilkins, otherwise called Colonel John Ticonderoga, the veteran, whose hoary locks were above described, and who had been the first to suggest to the others this laudable scheme.   Let those who take pride in such humble matters as dates and names, remember him, therefore, as the sixth leader of the choir at Waterfield, whose acts are recorded in this faithful chronicle.

My engagement in New Hampshire having expired, I returned home to pursue my studies.   Affairs had, by this time, assumed a much brighter aspect.   I found, on my arrival, that nearly all the females belonging to the late choir, had volunteered a renewal of their delightful services.   How difficult it is for woman to persevere in error !   Though, physically speaking, the weaker party, yet how often she resists the sinister example of the other sex, and proves herself superior in the strength of her moral powers. The fair ones of my native parish were the first to perceive the unhappy mistake into which they had been betrayed, and the first to acknowledge and practically retract it. Candour requires me to make these statements and reflections, though it were much to be wished that the occasion for it never had existed. But I was willing to forget all the resentment with which I had before wondered at their conduct, when I contemplated the novel and beautiful spectacle that now charmed my imagination. Show me a more interesting picture than reverend and trembling age associated with blooming and youthful beauty in chanting the praises of their common Creator. It struck me as an instance of a kind of *moral counterpoint*, more thrilling to the soul than the sweetest or the grandest harmony of mere sound. Willingly would I have refrained from interposing my indifferent voice, had not duty and persuasion united to re-conduct me to the seats.

The experience of life certainly brings every man into strange combinations and juxta-positions with his fellow beings. Yet, was not mine at the present time rather peculiar ? What fate, what hidden sympathy, what kindred gravity of character, drew me into special personal contact and cooperation with four of the most reverend seniors of the land ? The contemplation of this new attitude of my presiding genius, had sometimes almost too powerful an effect on my imagination. I began to entertain doubts of my own age. At times I thought it my duty to study a new system of ethics and manners, corresponding to my situation. I wished occasionally that Cicero's Treatise on Old Age might be substituted in place of his Orations against Catiline, which I was then reading, as preparatory to my admission into college.

But the dreams of this whimsical hallucination soon fled away, as the months advanced, and Mr Welby's voice regained its usual health and mellowness, and my

venerated fathers in harmony found it too
much for their comfort to ascend the stairs
on the enfeebling days of spring. Besides,
if any thing could have restrained the peculiar wanderings of my mind above described,
it was the condition in which I was now
left. Exposed singly to the fire of a whole
battery of eyes and voices from the flower
of the parish, and compelled, by my very
duty, to maintain constant communications
and consultations with them, I was soon
reminded, by certain indescribably interesting and perplexing feelings in my breast,
that I had many years yet to pass, before I
could aspire to the honours, the abstracted
attention, and the composure of old age.

But though I pretend not to have been
exempt from the susceptibilities now alluded
to, I call on every scrutinizing spectator,
(there having been several of that character
at church) to bear witness to the unremitted
propriety of my deportment during the summer and autumn which I passed in that
critical situation. No manifestation of par-

tialities, no encouragement of female frivoli-
ties, and no unfeeling neglect or inattention,
that I have ever heard of or imagined, were
or could be laid to my charge. Our singing,
I may confidently say without undue self-
flattery, continued to be of no ordinary
merit, though we could not welcome one
accession to my own side of the choir.
Several strong and rich voices on the other
side, took the tenor or air of each tune, the
rest of them united in a melodious treble,
and Mr Welby and myself put forth our
whole vocal powers in supporting them with
the bass. Such was the uninterrupted meth-
od we pursued, until the approach of winter
again called me to a distant place, to replen-
ish my little funds with the emoluments of
a district schoolmaster.

The destinies of our choir were now provided for in a manner, somewhat remarkable,
but not, I believe, altogether unexampled
elsewhere in our country. The first inten-
tion of the ladies was to leave the seats
immediately after my departure. Had it

been executed, every thing might have been thrown back into the deplorable condition in which I had left affairs the preceding winter. Two of my late venerable fellow choristers were now already gathered to the land of silence, and there were no hopes of obtaining a leader from any quarter. In this emergency, Mrs Martha Shrinknot proffered her services, and undertook the management of the whole department, until I should myself return and resume it. She was a lady, not much past the age of thirty years. Being of an active and inquisitive turn of mind, she had long since made herself acquainted with the mysteries of setting a psalm tune, knew its key note at a glance, and had frequently, on private occasions, even before her marriage, given out the leading tones to the different parts, when passing an evening with a few musical friends, who preferred extracting an hour of rational pleasure from the Village Harmony, to the frivolous entertainments of cards, coquetry, and scandal.

It might be out of place here, to follow Mrs Martha Shrinknot home, and exhibit her superintending the best ordered family, and the most profitable dairy in the county. My concern with her now is in her public capacity, and I may say with truth, that a leader of more accuracy, more judgment, more self-possession, and more spirited energy, never took charge of the Waterfield choir, nor, as I think, of any other choir.

Her outset on the first Sabbath succeeded to admiration ; and there was every prospect that her reign, though short, would be one of uninterrupted brilliancy and felicity. But an ill star seemed to hover over the spot, and new troubles soon arose to disturb the peace and crush the hopes of the lovers of sacred song.

Among the females of the choir, was a young woman of much comeliness, modest demeanour, and an unsullied character, who had been living in one of the richer families of the village, under the denomination of *help*. I approve the feeling which has substituted this word for the offensive one of *servant*. Servant seems to stamp an irretrievable character on the person who bears the appellation. It is less general and vague than the word help. The latter seems to admit into the mind a sense of independence and a hope of rising in the world. As long as Mirabeau's maxim is true, that names are things, let the young heirs of poverty and dependence in free America, solace themselves with the substantial comfort of assuming a title, which places them, in imagination at least, on a level with their employers, and soothes the sting which may now and then fret their bosoms, when contemplating the unavoidable inequalities of fortune. For alas ! not even will this slight change of name secure them from numerous embarrassments and mortifications, as will be seen in the case of Mary Wentworth, the intelligent young woman abovementioned.

The singing-pew for the females contained three long benches, rising one above another, and receding from the front of the gallery. Mary Wentworth had occupied an unassuming seat on the uppermost of these benches for about three years. At her first appearance there, there had been no little stir among certain of the vocal sisterhood; a few airs were put on; a few whispers circulated; a few stares directed at the modest stranger; and the seats of some of the young ladies were vacated for a few succeeding Sabbaths. But most of them returned sooner or later on better reflection, or on a reviving desire to bear their part in the melodies of the place, and Mary thenceforward was scarcely disturbed by any kind of notice whatever. Nevertheless, her singing was envied by some, and admired by all. To say the truth, she had no equal in this parish, and few elsewhere. Her voice was enchanting in its tones, and astonishing in its compass. She was a perfect mistress of the art, as far as it can reach perfection in the practice of our country choirs. She was fit to bear a conspicuous part in an oratorio, and would have well repaid any degree of scientific cultivation.

Mrs Shrinknot, who knew not, or affected not to know the squeamishness respecting rank, that was entertained by some of the young ladies, took occasion, on the afternoon of the second Sabbath succeeding her induction into office, to exercise her lawful authority, by inviting Mary Wentworth down to the front seat, and placing her at her own right hand. She wished for the support of her voice, and the assistance to be derived from occasionally consulting her.

On the next Sunday, Mrs Shrinknot was seized with an illness which prevented her leaving home. She sent for Mary, and after much persuasion, prevailed upon her to go that day and assume the direction of the choir.

The maiden went early, that she might prepare herself, by time and meditation, with sufficient self-possession, and avoid the flurry of passing by others in order to arrive at the post which had been assigned her. She

had not been seated there long, when she
observed two young ladies, who had for
some years pretty regularly attended the
choir, entering into a pew below with the rest
of their family. This was soon followed by
several other instances of the same kind,
and poor Mary's heart began to sink within
her. She looked frequently and anxiously
round, in the hope that some, or at least
that one individual would arrive to shield
her from the oppression of overwhelming notoriety. In vain! there had been visitings,
and murmurings, and resolutions, through
the whole of the preceding week, and what
with the pride of some, who could not endure that a girl at service should aspire at
an equality with themselves,—and the envy
of others, whose ears were *pained*, (as they
used to say, though in a different sense from
my use of the word,) with the tones of Polly
Wentworth's voice,—and the indignation of
others, that the long established order of
sitting should be disturbed,—and the pusil-
lanimity of others, who had neither souls

nor pretensions large enough to be proud, or
envious, or angry, but who quivered on the
pivot, and vibrated to whichever side the
multitude inclined,—not a bonnet was forth-
coming to gladden the eyes of that fair and
desolate housemaid.

Yet, though a girl of the most modest,
and unpretending character, Mary Wentworth had an energy of soul, and a sterling
good sense which enabled her to encounter
every emergency with composure, and to
act according to the demands of the occasion. Mr Welby, after waiting a quarter of
an hour beyond the usual time, and not
knowing himself, poor man, what course he
ought to pursue, balancing between his fear
of hurting the young woman's feelings, and
his duty as a clergyman, at length resolved
to commence the services with a psalm,
which he read, and proceeded to sing to the
tenor-part of a tune, that happened to be
the universal favourite of the congregation.

Mary Wentworth rose and joined him in
the same part. Mr Welby immediately

permitted his voice to slide, with a graceful and almost imperceptible transition, to the bass, with which he continued to accompany her. The air was of a slightly pathetic description, and thus accorded well with the state of her heart. To say that there was not a *little* effervescence of republican feeling, also, which prompted her, on that occasion, to put forth the whole blazing extent of her musical powers, would be, to arrogate for the fine creature a sort of angelical perfection, and to raise a doubt, whether the institutions, for which our fathers bled, have communicated to every one who moves over the land, a sense of individual dignity and importance. Yet, although grief and resentment were both labouring at her heart, her strength of character, and her instinctive perception of the proprieties of the place, suffered no more of either to predominate, than was exactly sufficient to infuse into her performance that combination of melancholy and animation, which is the last golden accomplishment of the female voice.

In fact, she was surprised at the excellence of her own singing, and this very surprise constantly stimulated her to higher and higher efforts. Her situation and feelings inspired new powers, of which she was unconscious before, and inspiration seemed to create and follow inspiration, like the metaphysical loves in the bosom of Anacreon.

The effect on the audience was prodigious. At first, there reigned the silence of astonishment that she could summon the confidence to sing. This was very soon exchanged for the feeling and the rustling of admiration. A kind of anguish now seized upon the hearts of some of the generous young ladies who had that morning left the choir. They were half willing to be back again there, if for no other purpose than to drown her voice, and dilute the attention so lavishly and improperly bestowed on a human being in the place of worship.

But the impropriety of this admiration appeared to be forgotten by even the gravest and most devout among the audience. As

Mary and the pastor proceeded from verse
to verse, one after another of their male lis-
teners rose, and turned their faces towards
the gallery, so that by the time the psalm
was concluded, and Mr Welby had laid
aside his book, to invite his people, in a low
and solemn tone, to the worship of God, one
half of the assembly were already in the
posture assumed by congregationalists, after
the manner of primitive christians, in the
hour of public prayer.

From seeming evil is educed real good.
The general compassion and admiration excited by the case of Mary Wentworth, now
presented an opportunity which had been
long desired among the singers of the other
sex, to return with a good grace to the seats.
By going thither again, ostensibly for the
purpose of encouraging and protecting a
persecuted young woman, they would screen
themselves from the mortification of appear-
ing to regret and retract their former conduct.   Accordingly, a deputation of ten, on
the afternoon of this day, resorted to the

spot in the capacity of harbingers or pioneers.
In consequence of the continued illness of
Mrs Shrinknot, the females generally declined to follow their example, entertaining
in their minds an insurmountable objection
against submitting to the substitute whom
she had appointed, notwithstanding the over-
flow of popularity that was now pouring towards that substitute. Not a lady, therefore, was to be seen ascending the stairs in
the afternoon, with the exception of Mary
herself, who came and resumed her former
long-occupied seat on the most retired bench
in the singing-pew, from which, no entrea-
ties, or arguments, or considerations, urged
by Mrs Shrinknot or others, could ever after induce her to remove. The noble girl
saw the hopelessness of contending against
a host of jealous and restless prejudices,
and cared for nothing in that place, so much
as peace and good singing.

Mr Welby was still obliged to act as precentor during the remainder of the day.
The new recruits for the vocal service, the

sight of whom gladdened his heart, felt un-
equal to the task of executing that function
among themselves. After he had read the
first psalm in the afternoon, and they had
waited some time for him to begin the singing of it, he perceived what was wanting,
and speedily commenced a tune. He did
the same with the two other hymns for that
day. Mary would instantaneously take the
treble, and her companions joined her, one
after another, according as they could seize
the parts belonging to them. After a few
trifling mistakes in the bass, which the good
ears, however, of those who committed them,
were able immediately to correct, they succeeded in making themselves all masters of
the air before the conclusion of the first
verse, and then proceeded with tolerable
spirit and correctness .to the end of the
hymn.

On my return home, I had the felicity to
find the choir in a more flourishing condition
than it had enjoyed for a long time. About
twenty of my own sex occupied the octago-

nal box, and somewhat less than that number
were induced by the recovery and presence
of Mrs Shrinknot, and the prudent humility
of Mary, to fill the two lower seats of the
adjoining pew. These were all in the best
training possible under the management of
the former powerful lady, who, on receiving
the keynote from the bachelor-merchant's
bass-viol, immediately sounded forth the
melodious fall of fa, sol, la, fa, and distributed the leading notes round to the performers
of each of the four parts ;—that complement being sometimes effected by an animated counter from the lips of Mary Wentworth.

From this time until the succeeding autumn, when I entered college, I discharged
the duties of chief singer without interruption. It was a smoothly spun and brightly
dyed portion of the thread of my life. The
choir was making constant improvements,
and receiving now and then accessions
to its numbers, as was to be expected from
the exercise of regularity and perseverance
in the main body.

Very few occurrences happened to disturb the full cup of satisfaction which I was now enjoying in peace and gratitude. I cannot, however, omit mentioning one momentary dash of bitter, that was casually mingled with its sweets. In the middle of Mr Welby's long prayer, one July morning, the composure of the congregation was startled by the loud crack of a whip before the meetinghouse. Two or three of the younger members of the choir immediately rushed on tip-toe out of the singing seats to the windows, from which they beheld a gig and tandem approaching rapidly to the door, and saw a pair of gaily dressed gentlemen alight therefrom. In a moment after, we heard the confident and conscious footsteps of their creaking yellow-top boots ascending the stairs, and on turning my eyes, but not my body in that direction, whom should I behold but my old acquaintance and competitor Mr Forehead, accompanied by a gentlemanly-looking friend ? They had ridden that morning from Boston, where Mr Fore-

head was a successful attorney of much re-
pute in * * * * * Alley. They both came
into the octagonal pew with the same unem-
barrassed freedom that they would have
entered a bar-room, and took the first vacant
seats in their way ; but on reconnoitring,
and finding everybody around them in a
standing posture, they exchanged smiles of
some confusion with each other, and arose
again. From Mr Forehead's familiar nod
to me, I should have thought I had seen him
but yesterday, instead of parting with him
full two years before. I should have returned it with a solemn bow, had not the
service which Mr Welby was now performing made it improper for me to bestow on
him the slightest recognition. Their assistance in the tune which soon succeeded, was
very fine, and very acceptable to the choir
and congregation. They joined us again,
however, in the afternoon, and while we
were singing the first psalm, they thought
proper instead of lending us their voices, to
accompany us with a singular *stridor*, emitted

through the nearly closed lips, and resembling something between the sound of a bassoon, and the lowest tone of a bass-viol. Some of the choir were frightened, some were shocked, and some very nearly burst out with laughter. My own distress was inconceivable. I felt *haunted* by Mr Forehead. Rendered absolutely disheartened at the thought of enduring that sacrilegious, though I confess not entirely inharmonious buzz through the two remaining hymns, I retired from the meetinghouse and went home. Mr Forehead immediately assumed my office, for the afternoon, and his friend, at the request of Mrs Shrinknot, exchanged his imitative experiments for more natural and appropriate tones.

This, however, was the most disagreeable episode in the present poetic period of my existence. It is doubtful whether at length the separation from my own family, caused me a keener pang, than the thought that I must resign, and perhaps forever, all connexion with a little circle, in which I had lately enjoyed, to so eminent a degree, the double privilege of receiving happiness and doing good.

After my departure, a variety of causes, unnecessary to be detailed, contributed to the gradual decline and ultimate extinction of the choir on its old foundation. My shorter college-vacations I spent at home, and in vain endeavoured to arrest this melancholy tendency by the few exertions I could make to rally the scattered members. Sometimes I found that a miserable kind of contest had been waged between Mrs Shrinknot, and the singers of the other sex, who made all the efforts in their power to emancipate themselves from the mortifying dominion of a woman. But they could never succeed, not a man among them possessing sufficient tact, knowledge, and presence, to carry off the business of a leader well. The singing was always decent under her management, but under theirs, it was perpetually liable to mistakes, interruptions, languishments, and helpless amazements. There was, however, no open, clamorous warfare between the two parties, but only on one side the restless attempts of pride to repair its own mortifications, and on the other the calm defiance of conscious superiority. They avoided an actual clashing before the congregation. The lady always affected a perfect readiness to yield her authority, whenever there were gentlemen present who chose to set the psalm. But this state of things of course produced frequent embarrassments in the choir. The bowings and the consultations between Mrs Shrinknot and the gentlemen, occasioned by doubts respecting the propriety of particular tunes and other matters, were frequently protracted long after the minister had read the psalm or hymn, and the congregation would sit waiting and wondering for the music to begin. Meanwhile, as was to be expected, several of the least zealous members of the choir, would from time to time steal off from their duties, to sit below, rather than be witnesses and partakers of such pitiable scenes.

FROM:

TO:

GARY LIBRARY
VERMONT COLLEGE
MONTPELIER, VT 05602

ADDRESS SERVICE REQUESTED

MAY BE OPENED FOR POSTAL INSPECTION IF NECESSARY

_____ PARCEL POST   _____ EXPRESS COLLECT
_____ PREINSURED   _____ EXPRESS PREPAID
$_____ VALUE

DEMCO

The prosperity of my former hobby was still further affected by the introduction of theological perplexities. A flaming young preacher, who carried some points of orthodoxy considerably further than I could then, or can even now approve, had been recently settled in a neighbouring town, and exchanged services one Sabbath with Mr Welby. Tall of stature, cadaverous in aspect, and gloomy in his address as the very depths of midnight, he arose, and after pausing three minutes, during which his eyes were rivetted on his book, he gave out the forty fourth hymn of the Second Book of Dr Watts, in a voice a full octave below that tone which is commonly called the sepulchral.   The hymn is a terrific combination of images respecting the future abode of the wicked, and contains, among others of a similar nature the two following verses :

'Far in the deep where darkness dwells,
The land of horror and despair,
Justice hath built a dismal hell,
And laid her stores of vengeance there.

' Eternal plagues, and heavy chains,
Tormenting racks, and fiery coals,
And darts to inflict immortal pains,
Dy'd in the blood of damned souls ! '

On that day the person who undertook to act as leader of the choir, was a middle-aged tinplate-worker, who had recently become a warm convert to the doctrines of Universalism. There were a few of his own persuasion in the singing-seats, and there were some, who thought little of the matter either one way or the other, but who would gladly have excused themselves from singing the appointed lines, if others of a milder character could be substituted.

Mrs Shrinknot was born to be finally an ultra-religionist, but she had not yet taken her decided part in polemics. Her imagination had been much wrought upon at this very moment by the novel phenomenon in the pulpit. She was already an incipient convert ; already prepared to yield up her mind to the whole influence of his manner, and the whole demands of his doctrines.

When she perceived, therefore, that a majority of singers in the octagon had come to a resolution not to sing the forty fourth hymn, second book, nor even a single verse of it, her whole soul was inflamed with the spirit of personal and controversial opposition, and she has since dated her entire conversion from that moment. She turned round to Mary Wentworth, and requested her support, as she was about to rise and commence the hymn, in spite of the fixed resolutions of the other side of the choir. Mary shook her head with her usual firmness, and her friend appeared for a moment daunted. But at length when a sufficient time had elapsed to put the congregation out of all patience, and the young theologian had arisen again from his seat, and was leaning far over the cushion, with eyes prying into the gallery, to ascertain, if possible, the cause of the delay, Mrs Shrinknot, at the very moment of her rising to commence the hymn alone, was interrupted and astonished by the following dialogue which took place between

the tinplate-worker leaning over the gallery,
and the clergyman leaning over the pulpit.

Tinplate-worker.—'You are requested,
Reverend Sir, to give out another hymn.'

Minister.—'Why am I requested to do so,
Sir ?'

Tinplate-worker.—'We do not approve of
the sentiments of the hymn you have just
read.'

Minister.—'I decline reading any other.'

Tinplate-worker.—'Then we decline singing, Sir.'

Minister.—(After pausing some time with
a look of wretched anxiety, sorrow, indignation, and horror, at what he felt was a sacrilegious violation of his undoubted authority)
—'Let us pray.'

The congregation obeyed his direction, so
far as rising on their feet could be so doing ;
but had he said, ' Let us speculate on the
scene that has just occurred,' his exhortation
would have obtained a far more universal
compliance that day than is generally paid
to dictations from the sacred desk, and would

have corresponded with marvellous exactness to what actually rolled over and over in the minds of the audience, while the minister himself was beginning at the fall, and going through the whole body of divinity in his prayer, dwelling at much length and with peculiar emphasis on the most dreadful realities of the future world.

Of course, during the ensuing week, the parish was in an uproar. The communing members, technically called the church, who bore omnipotent sway in the internal affairs of the congregation, pressed upon Mr Welby the execution of this rule, viz : that he should begin at the beginning of Watts's Psalm Book on the next Lord's Day, and proceeding regularly through that book, cause every verse of every psalm and hymn without omission or exception to be sung in their existing order, and never should depart therefrom,—Watts, like the Common Prayer Book in the Church of England, receiving, in many parts of this region, an equal reverence with the Bible.

But the measures taken to secure sound doctrine, were ill-calculated to preserve good singing. From this moment my poor choir laboured with its death-wound. Occasionally considerable numbers would attend it, and even the tinplate-worker condescended to lend his services, when he could look forward and ascertain that the psalms for the day interfered not with his ultra-latitudinarian creed. But there was no system, no regularity, no zeal, none of that essential *esprit-de-corps*, which constitutes the very life of a band of singers. You could more easily calculate on the weather of an approaching Sabbath, than you could on its music. A visit of Mr Murray, the Universalist preacher, to the neighbourhood, was certain to draw three quarters of the choir away. Mary Wentworth departed to keep school at Hampton Falls. Mrs Shrinknot, disgusted with the moderation of Mr Welby, who has always satisfied myself with his mild orthodoxy, rode constantly several miles to attend the ministrations of the young divine, who had innocently caused an accelerated decay of the choir. A sense of the unfashionableness of singing at the meetinghouse, would at times pervade all the females of the village, and keep them for several months in their pews below. A hundred caprices, a hundred quarrels, rose one after another, in quicker succession, and of more paltry nature than I can permit myself to describe. The very knowledge of sacred music seemed to be fast decaying. No recruits from the rising generation prepared themselves as formerly to take part in this interesting portion of worship. No movement was started from any quarter to effect a better order of things. All classes were sunk in musical apathy. The Village Harmony and other Collections belonging to the seats, were carried off and never recovered. Many of the benches in the octagon were broken down by idle boys who went to overlook the doings of town-meetings, and were omitted to be repaired. A feeble attempt was generally made to sing once on each part of the

day, but that precariously depended on Mr
Welby's feelings and state of health.   And
if now and then a scattered worshipper or
two straggled into the seats, it was either
because they wished to change their places
at church for the mere sake of variety, or
because they could call no other spot their
own.

Such was the condition in which I found
the once flourishing singing-pew at Waterfield, when, after having passed four years
in Harvard College, and three in a lawyer's
office in the county of Bristol, I came and
nailed up a professional sign in the centre
of my native village.   On the first Sabbath,
instinct led me to the spot.   In going to the
meetinghouse, I confess I felt too much
complacency in the conscious improvement
which the preceding seven years had effected in my mind and person.   But, alas ! this
momentary infirmity was full severely pun-
ished, when, on approaching the singing-pew,
I perceived it too desolate and dusty to be
occupied.   I passed a mournful day ; but

better times and better things ere long arose,
which I may perhaps be able to recount at
some future period, when, (if my present
essay find favor with an indulgent public, and
my leisure from an increasing business permit,) I shall attempt the *History of a New
England Singing School.*